kids draw MANGA

CHRISTOPHER HART

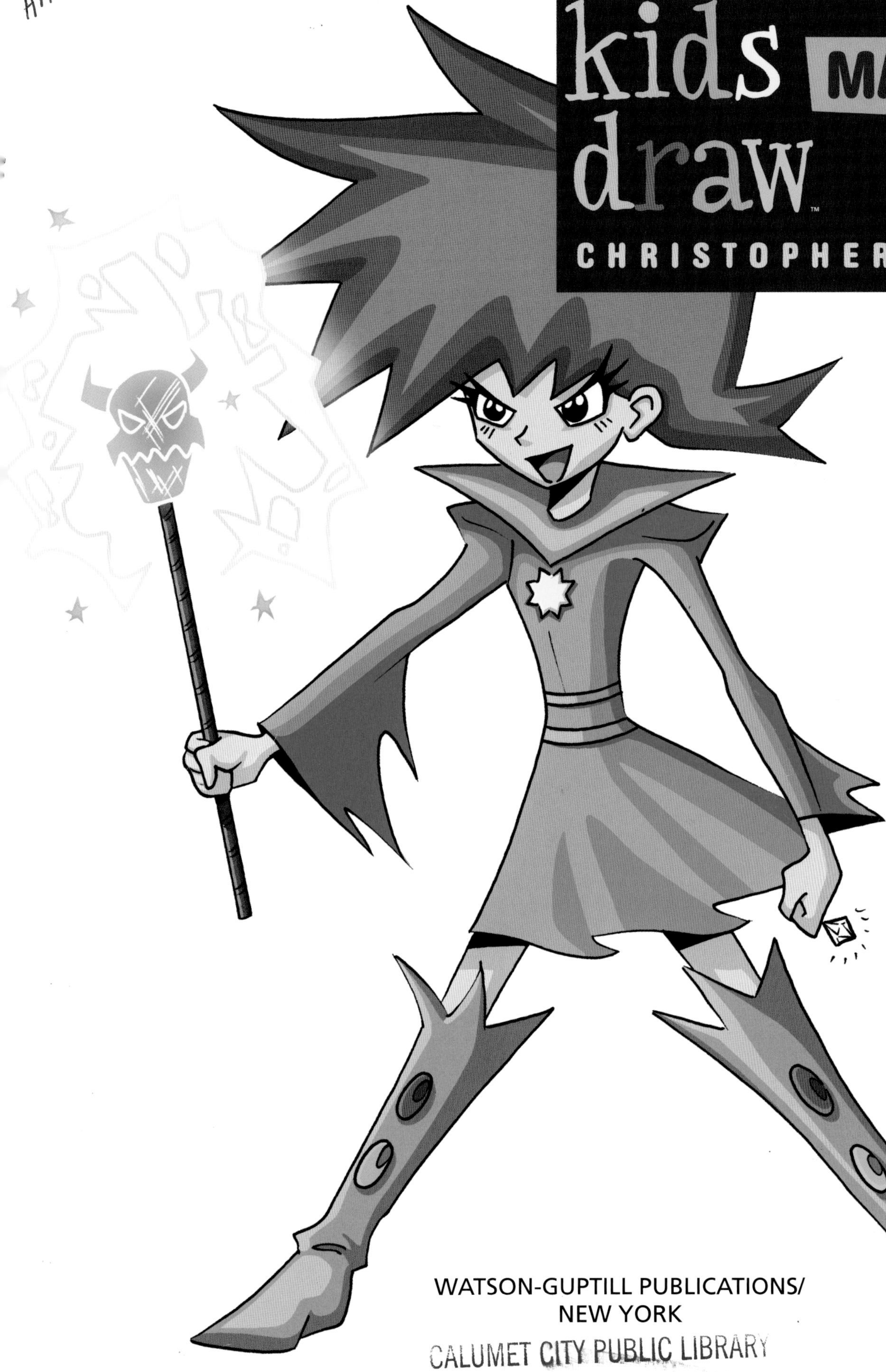

WATSON-GUPTILL PUBLICATIONS/
NEW YORK

Dedicated to
my readers

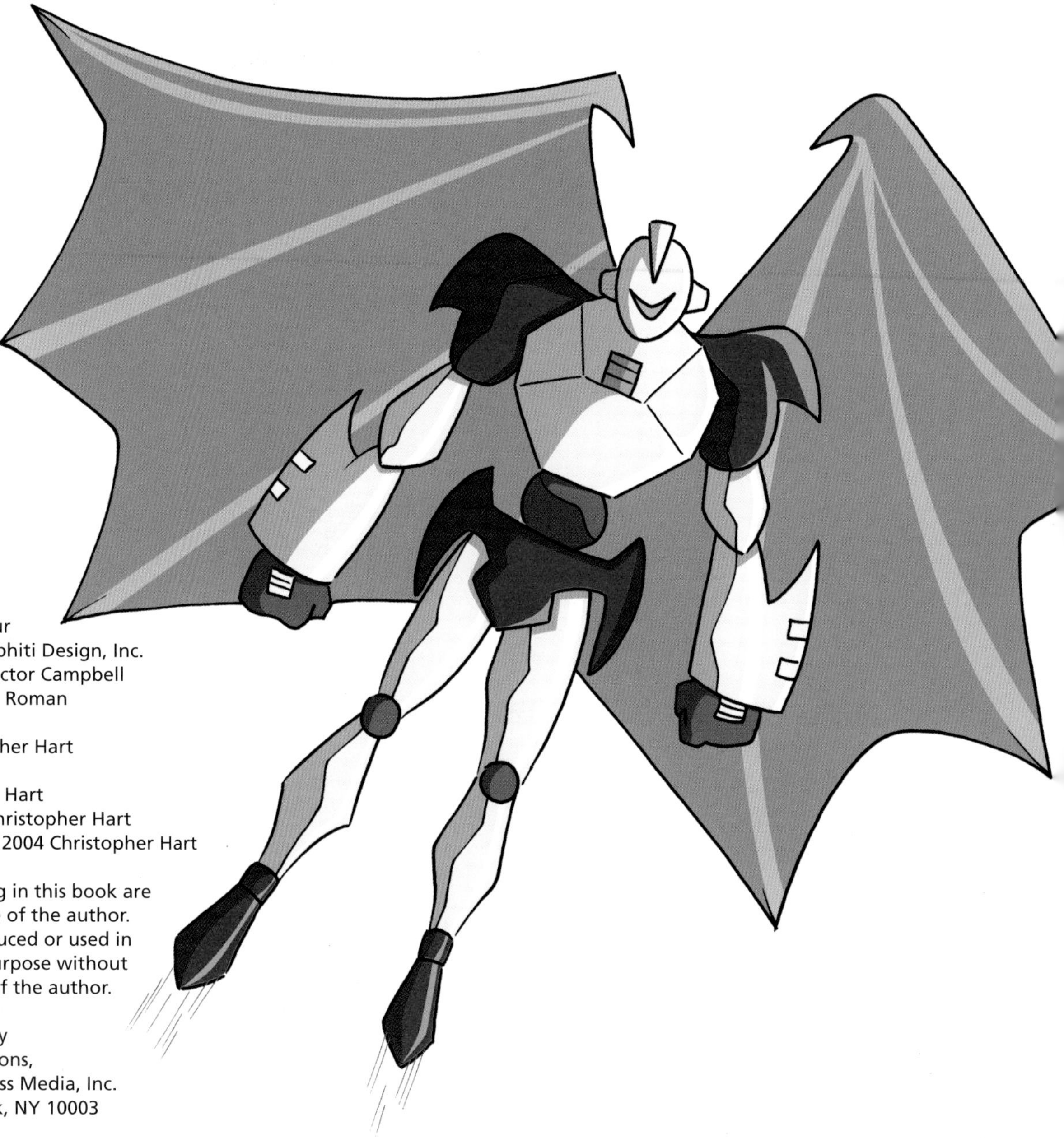

Senior Editor: Julie Mazur
Designer: Bob Fillie, Graphiti Design, Inc.
Production Manager: Hector Campbell
Text set in 12-pt Frutiger Roman

All drawings by Christopher Hart

Cover art by Christopher Hart

First published in 2004 by
Watson-Guptill Publications,
a division of VNU Business Media, Inc.
770 Broadway, New York, NY 10003
www.watsonguptill.com

Library of Congress Cataloging-in-Publication Data
Hart, Christopher.
Kids draw Manga / Christopher Hart.
p. cm. — (Kids draw)
Includes index.
ISBN 0-8230-2623-X
1. Comic books, strips, etc.—Japan—Technique—Juvenile literature.
2. Cartooning—Technique—Juvenile literature. I. Title.
NC1764.5.J3H36927 2004
741.5—dc22

2003019493

Printed in U.S.A.

First printing, 2004

2 3 4 5 6 7 8 / 11 10 09 08 07 06 05 04

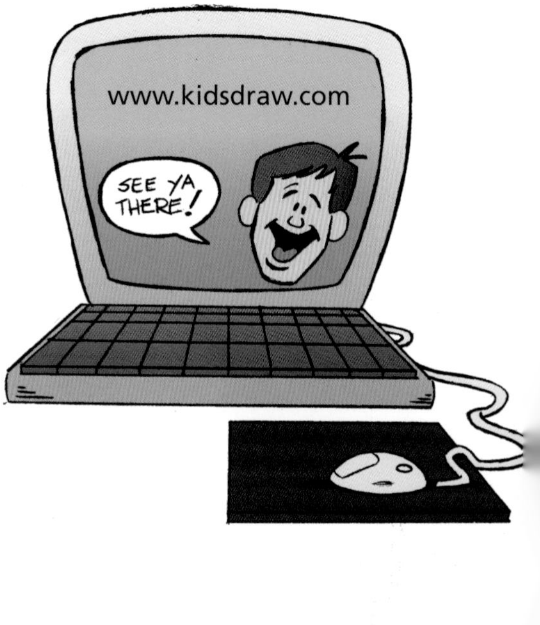
www.kidsdraw.com
SEE YA THERE!

CONTENTS

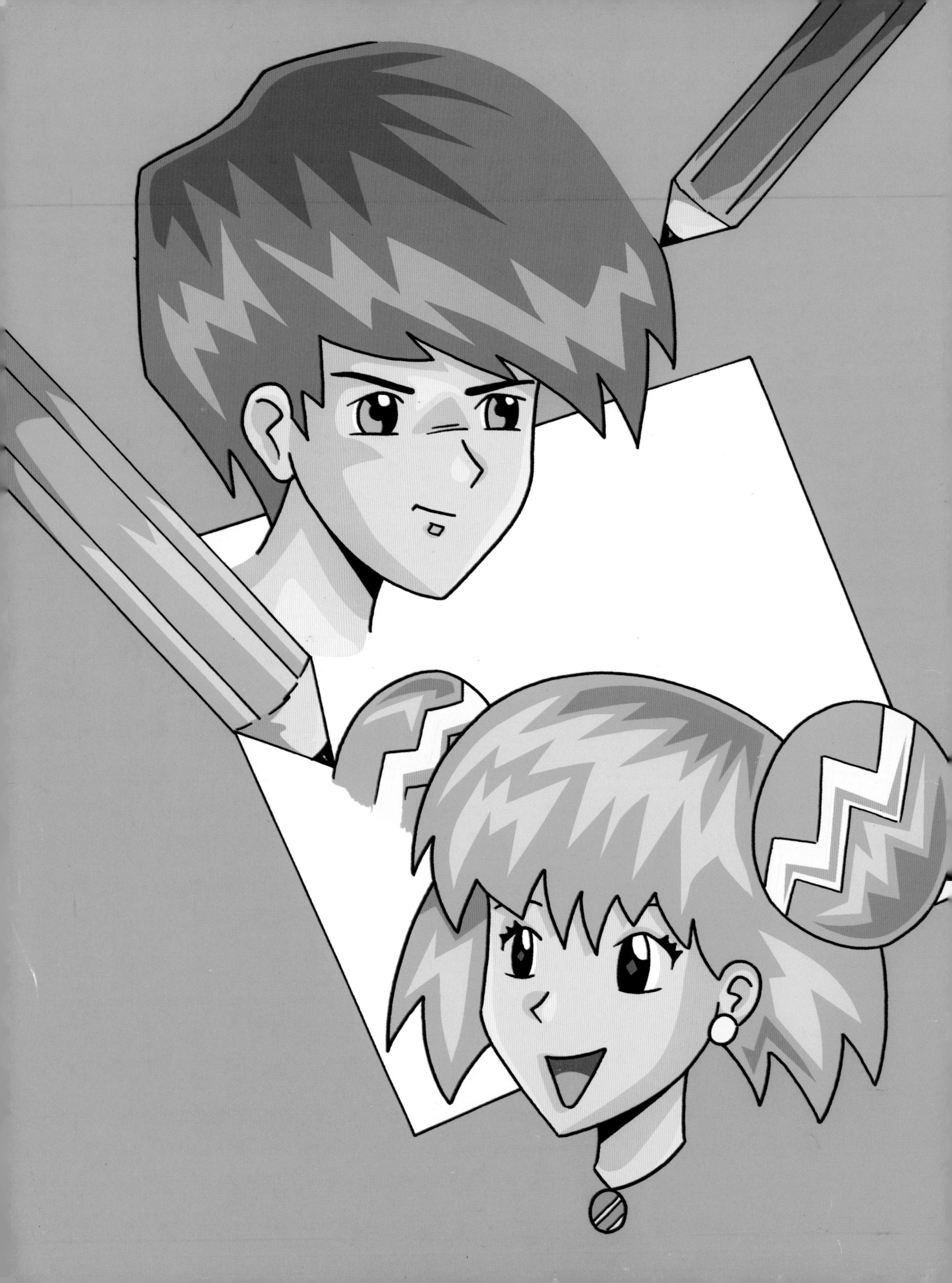

INTRODUCTION

Manga is a Japanese word that means "comics." We use it to describe Japanese-style comics. If you bought this book, you probably know that manga is the newest craze with kids, teens, and young adults. Everyone loves the big-eyed characters of manga! This book will teach you to do manga drawings so cool your friends will be begging to learn how you did them!

Kids Draw Manga will teach you everything you need to draw *authentic* manga. You'll start with the basics,

like how to draw manga-style faces and heads. Then you'll learn to draw a bunch of manga-style characters, from young boys and girls to intense sci-fi commanders and giant fighting robots.

Each drawing is broken down into easy steps that you can follow yourself. We'll start with simple characters, then move on to more complicated ones—this way, the book grows with you as you learn.

If you're a manga fan and you like to draw, get ready for hours and hours of creative fun!

MANGA BASICS

Let's get right to the good stuff! Take out a pencil and paper, and let's get started.

Drawing the Eye

The eyes are the most important part of any manga character. Draw them very big and round, with huge shines. There are at least two shines in the typical manga-style eye, sometimes even more.

BOY'S EYE

1. Draw the top eyelid.

2. Add the iris (the colored part of the eye).

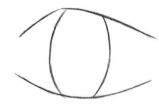

3. Draw the bottom eyelid.

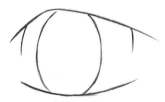

4. Show the inner and outer edges of the eye.

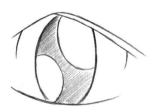

5. Add the upper eyelid crease and the "shines." Color in the iris.

6. Darken the iris. Leave the shines white.

GIRL'S EYE

Girls' eyes are drawn differently from boys' eyes. Most girls' eyes are drawn in the shape of a box.

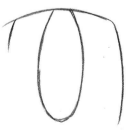

1. Start the outline of the eye. Add the iris.

2. Draw the bottom of the eye.

3. Draw the eyelashes.

4. Add the "shines" inside the iris.

5. Color in the eyelashes and the iris. Leave the shines white.

Now that you've seen how to draw the eye by itself, try adding a pair of eyes to a real manga face. Trace the head in step 1, then follow the other steps to add the eyes.

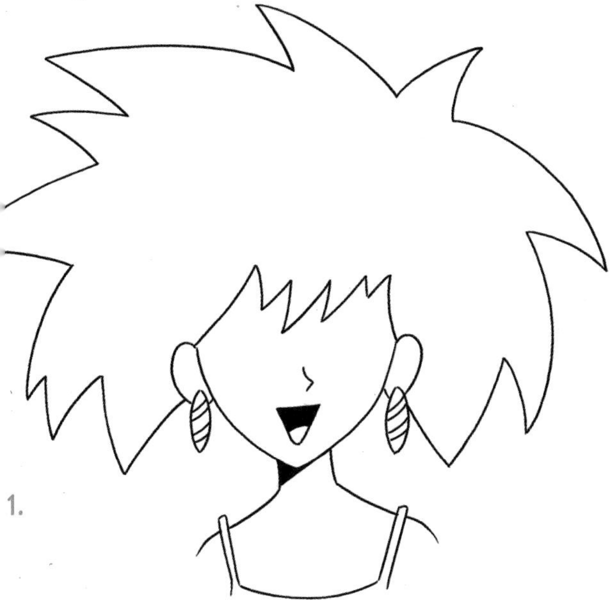

1.

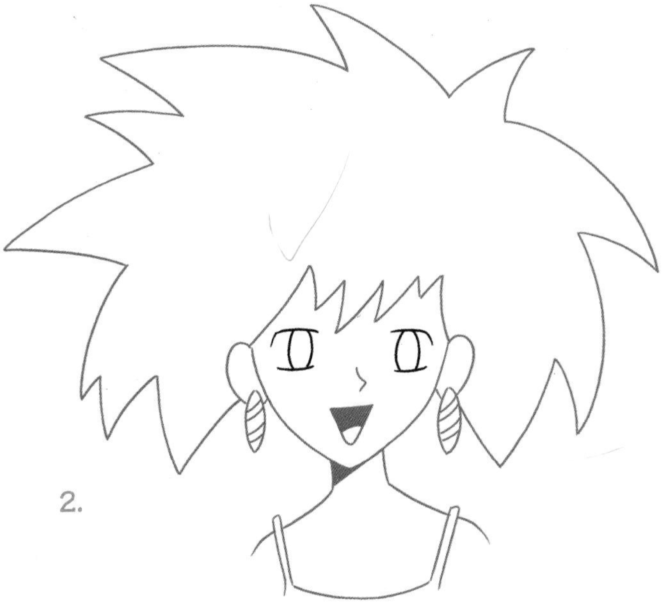

2.

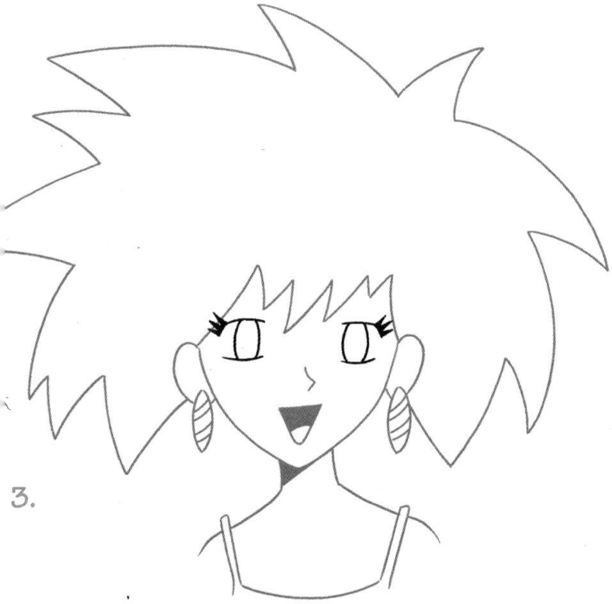

3.

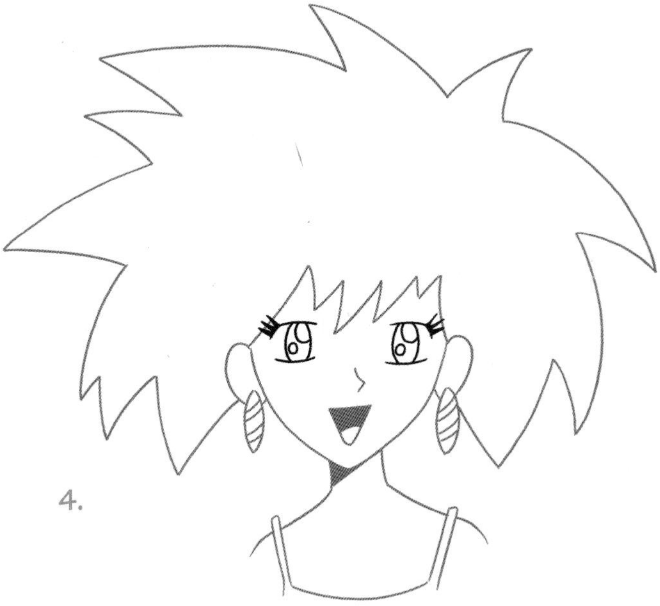

4.

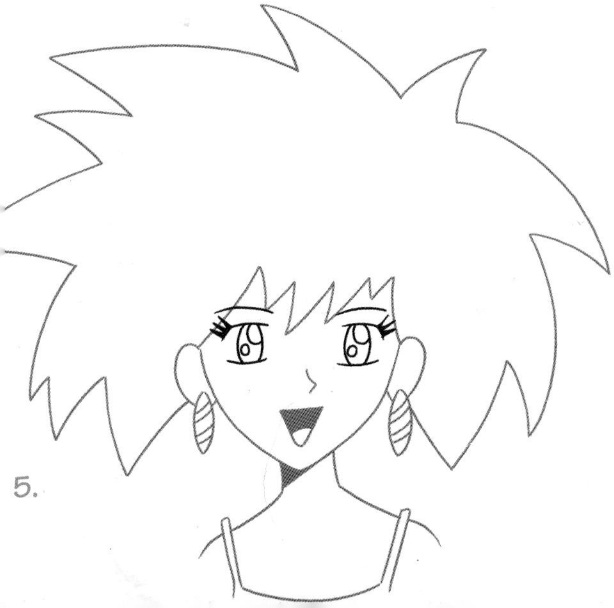

5.

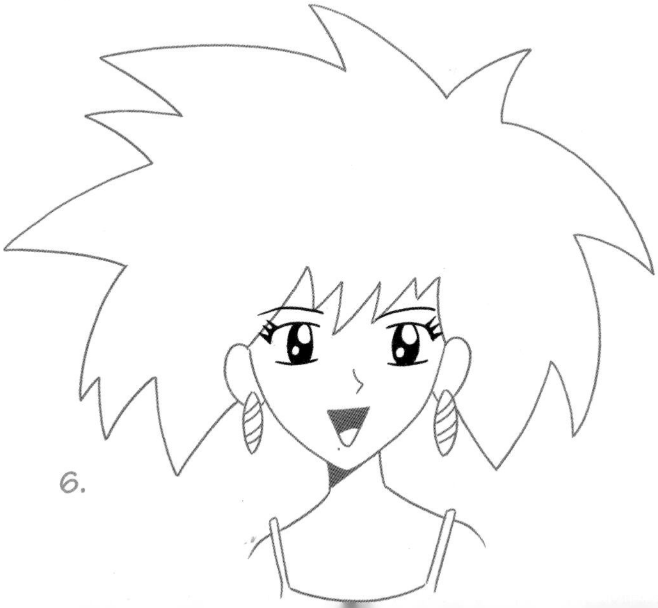

6.

Drawing the Mouth

Look at all of the different expressions you can create, just by changing the shape of the mouth. Here are a few typical mouth positions and some tips on drawing them.

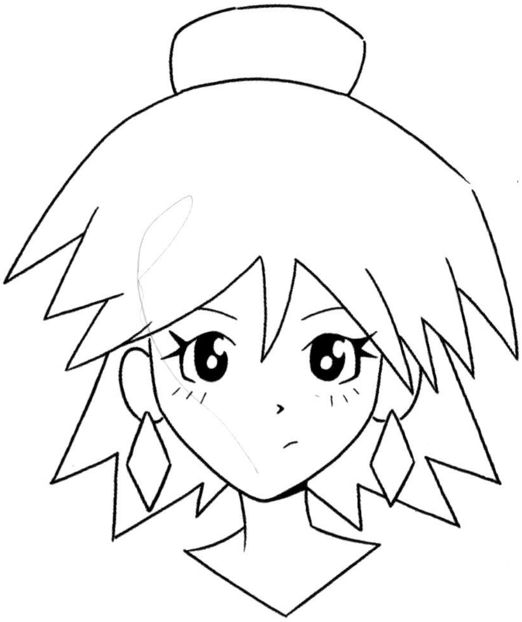

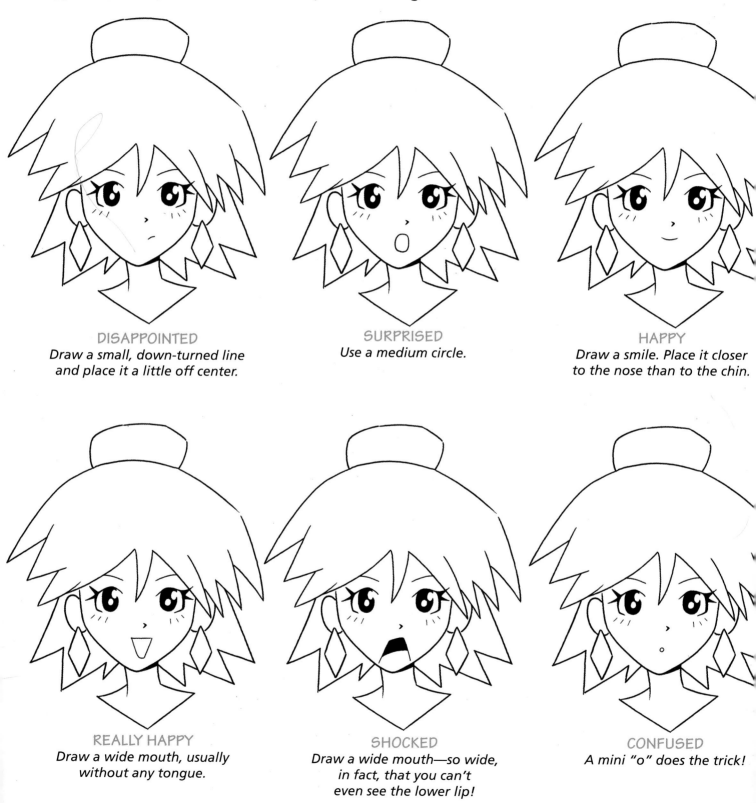

DISAPPOINTED

Draw a small, down-turned line and place it a little off center.

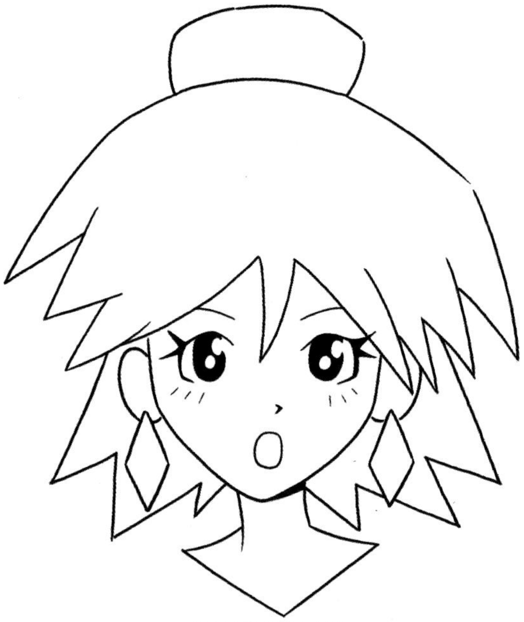

SURPRISED

Use a medium circle.

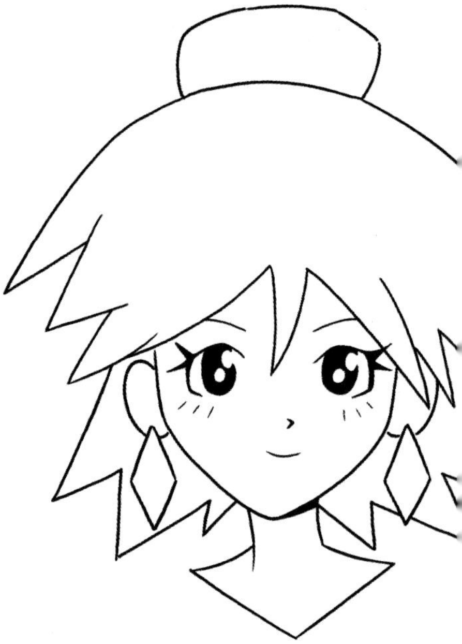

HAPPY

Draw a smile. Place it closer to the nose than to the chin.

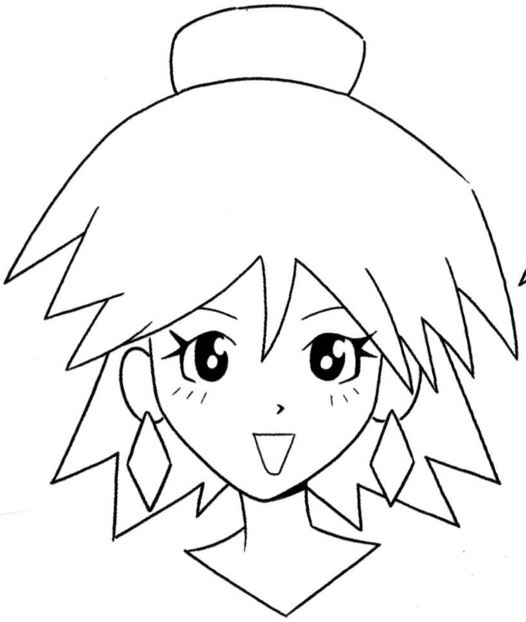

REALLY HAPPY

Draw a wide mouth, usually without any tongue.

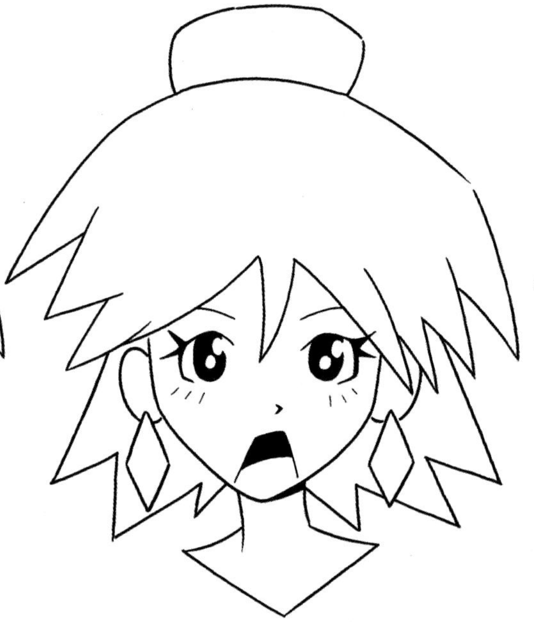

SHOCKED

Draw a wide mouth—so wide, in fact, that you can't even see the lower lip!

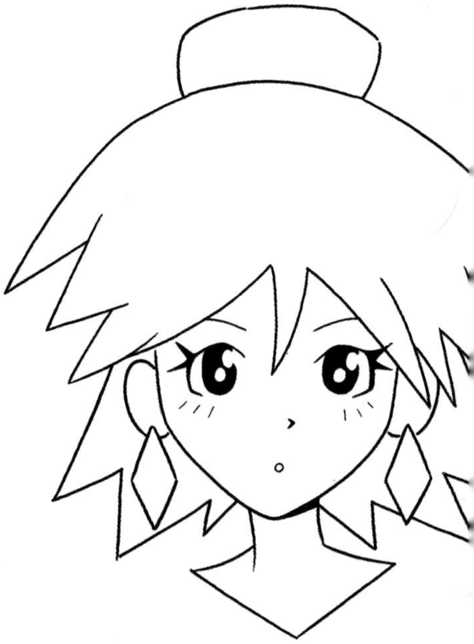

CONFUSED

A mini "o" does the trick!

Drawing the Nose

Manga characters have sharp noses that turn up at the end. Notice that as the head turns, the nose looks like it's changing shape. Here are a few rules to remember so you'll always get the nose right.

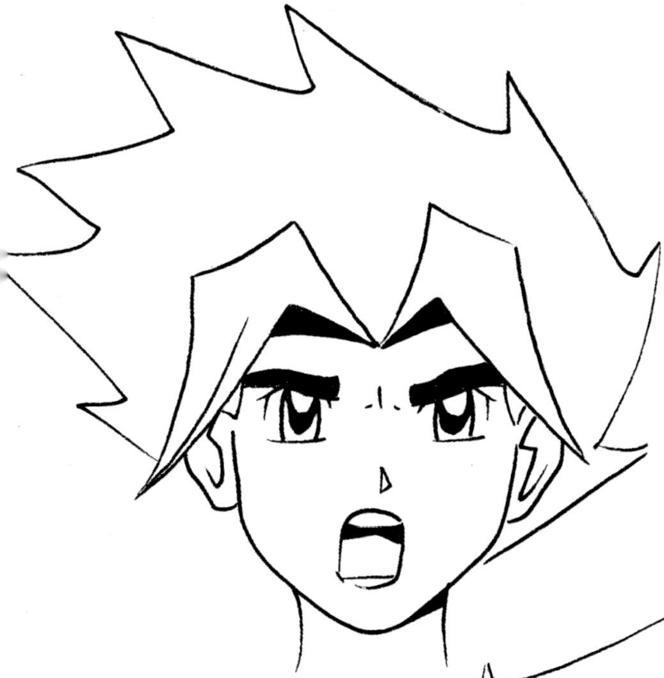

FRONT VIEW

For a front view, just draw the shadow that the nose casts. It looks like a thin triangle.

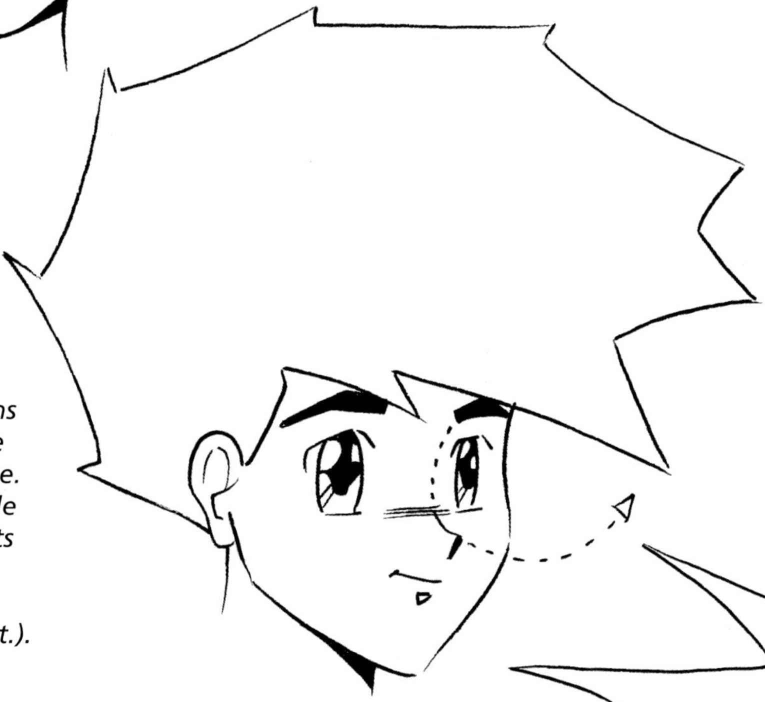

3/4 VIEW

As the character turns away, we start to see the shape of the nose. It's formed by a single curved line that starts at the far eyebrow (You don't have to draw the dotted part.).

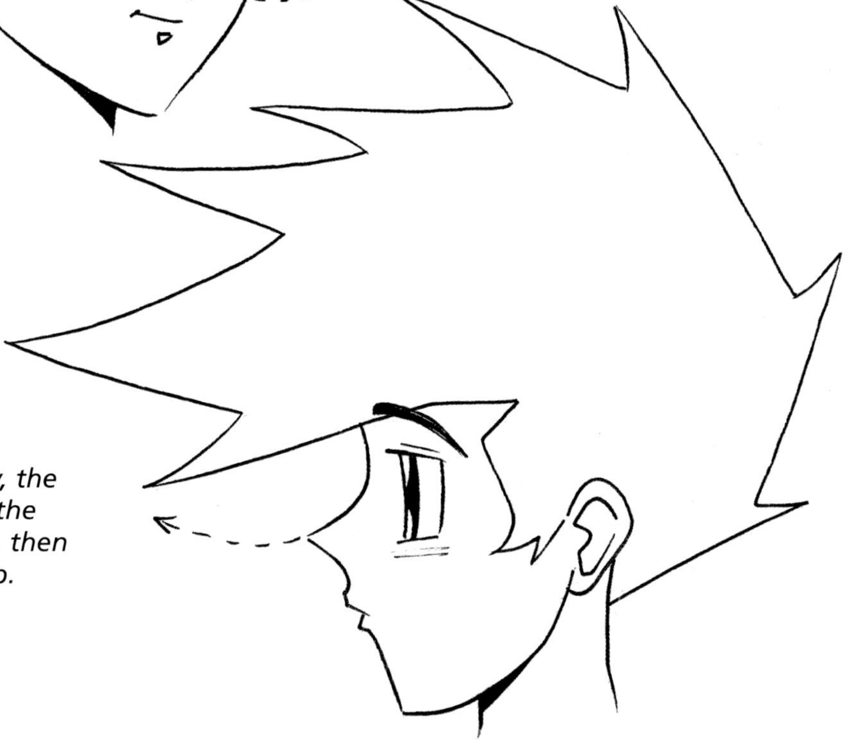

PROFILE

For a profile, or side view, the line of the nose starts at the forehead. It slopes down, then sweeps up, like a ski jump.

The Shape of the Head

Okay, so you've learned how to draw the eyes, nose, and mouth. Now you need a place to put them! Our next job is to tackle the overall shape of the manga-style head. Most manga heads have certain things in common.

BOY'S HEAD

Let's start with a typical manga boy's head. This one is a 3/4 view, which is halfway between a front view and a side view.

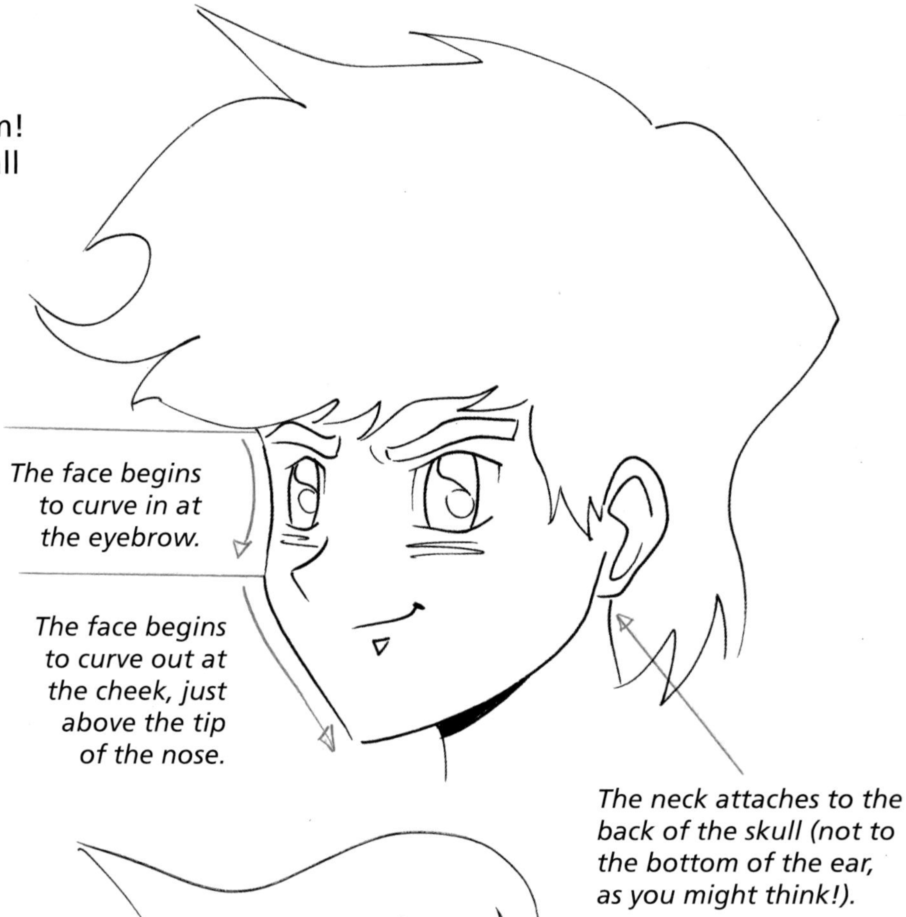

The face begins to curve in at the eyebrow.
The face begins to curve out at the cheek, just above the tip of the nose.
The neck attaches to the back of the skull (not to the bottom of the ear, as you might think!).

GIRL'S HEAD

Here is a front view of a typical girl. In manga, girls have very big hairstyles that make their heads look taller.

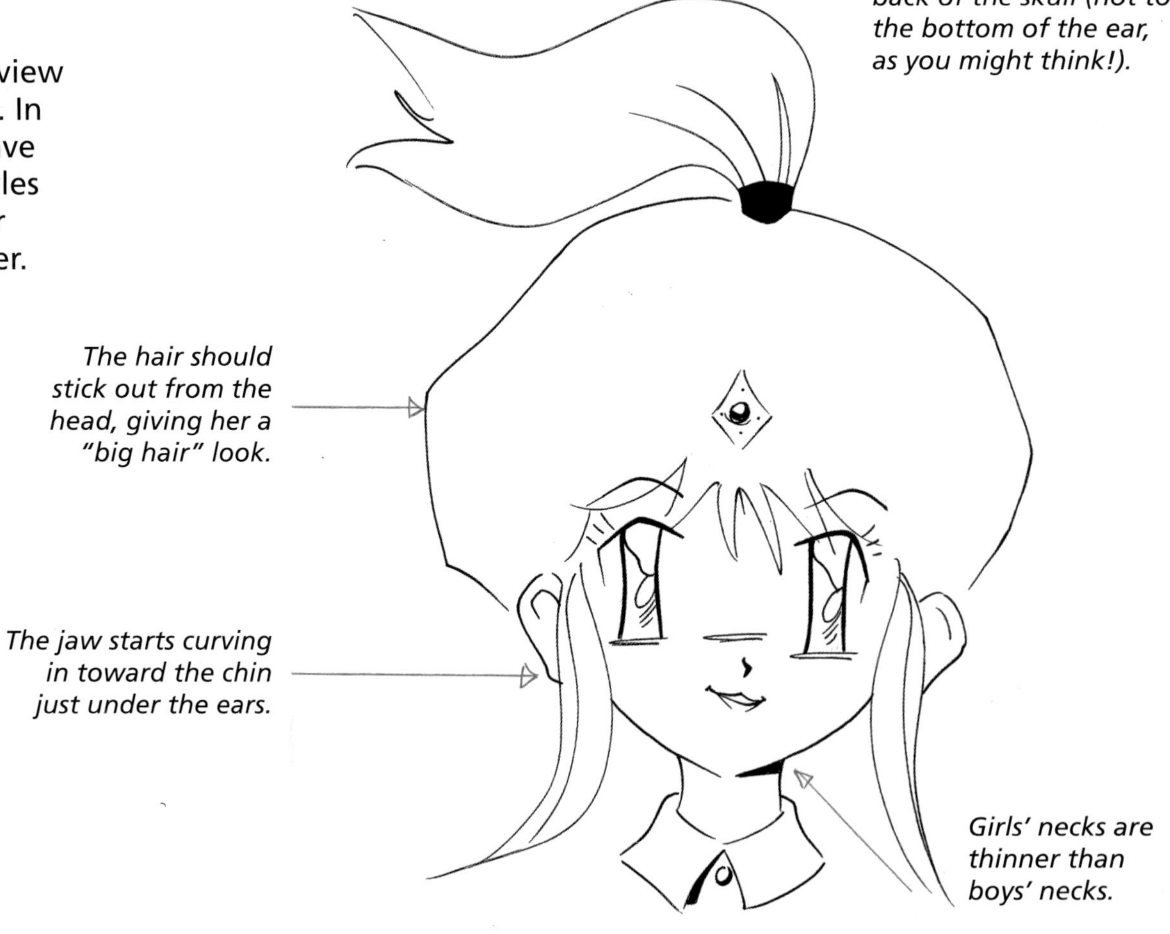

The hair should stick out from the head, giving her a "big hair" look.
The jaw starts curving in toward the chin just under the ears.
Girls' necks are thinner than boys' necks.

Tips and Tricks

Here are some tips that will help your drawings look professional.

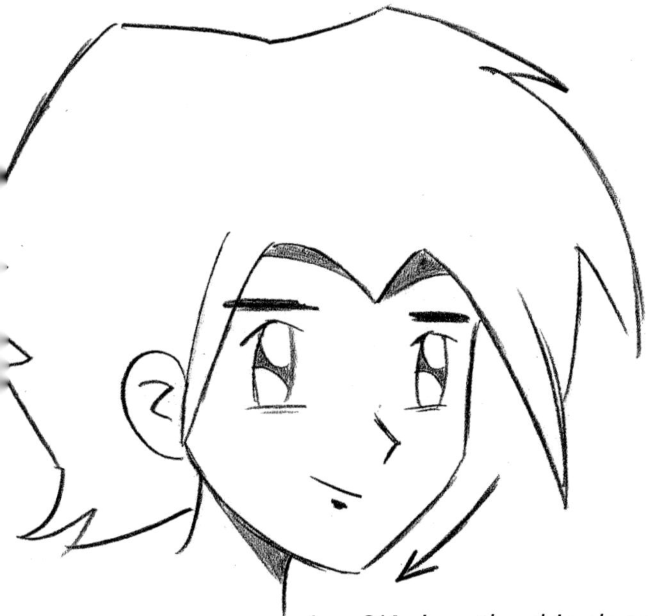

In a 3/4 view, the chin slopes back at a severe angle. Manga characters almost never have chins that stick out.

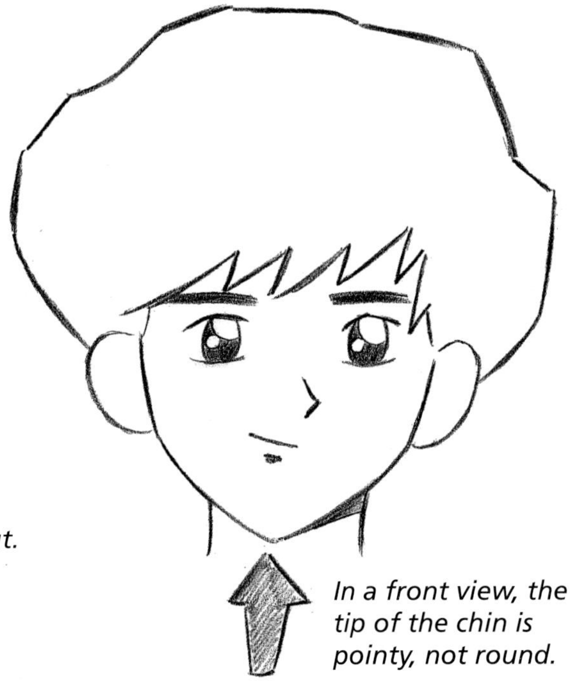

In a front view, the tip of the chin is pointy, not round.

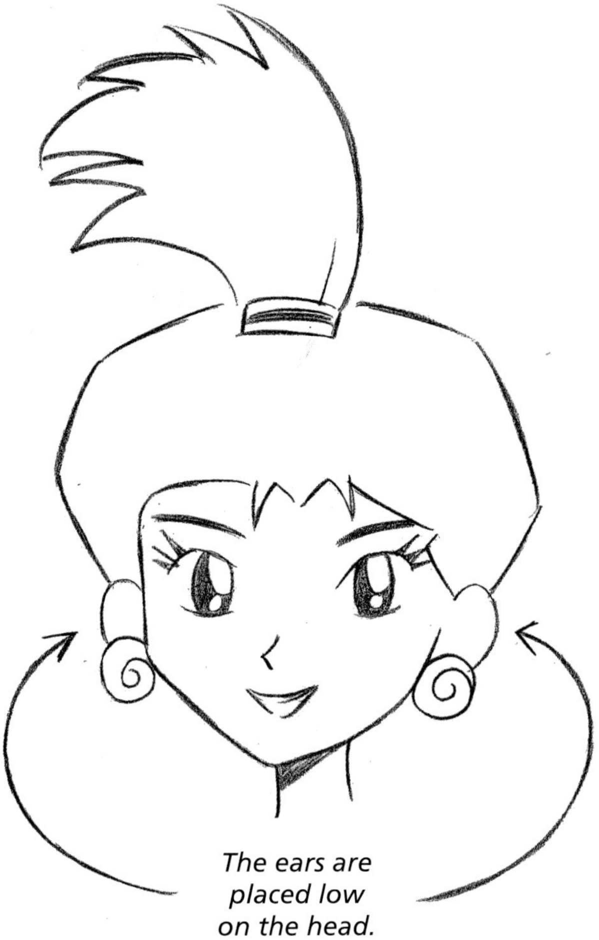

The ears are placed low on the head.

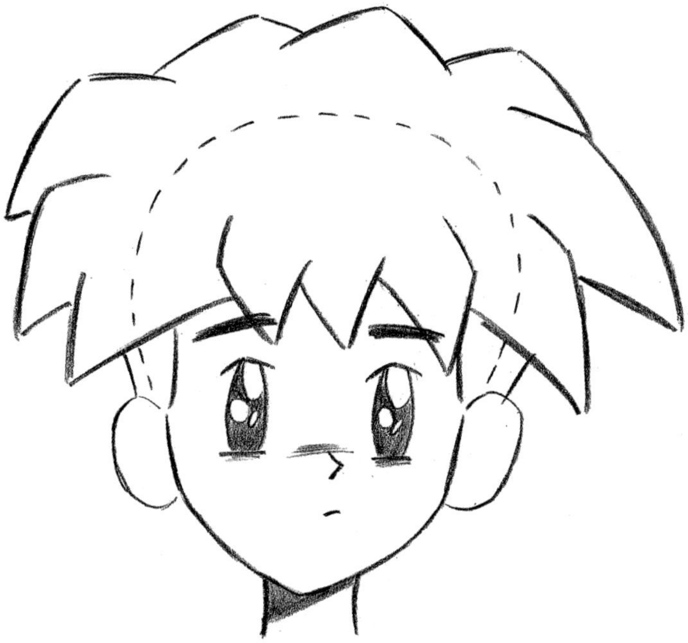

The top of the head is always large. This helps make the character look young.

Drawing the Body: Boys Versus Girls

Manga boys are usually drawn taller than manga girls. Also, the boy's upper body is straight, while the girl's upper body changes shape. The girl's body is wide at the shoulders, narrow at the waist, and wide at the hips. The girl's shoulders are usually wider than her waist, which helps make her look young.

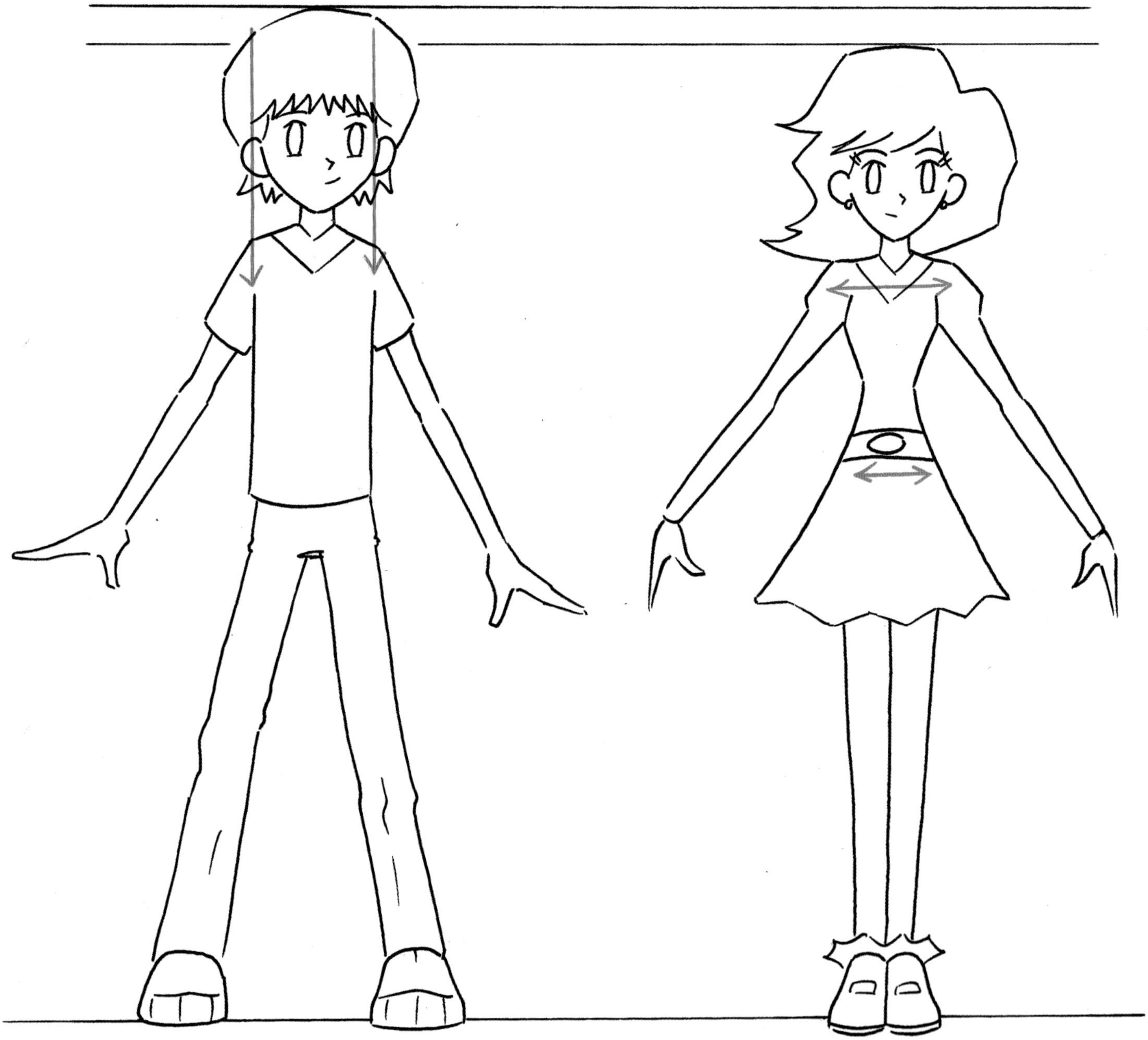

Dividing the Body into Sections

These drawings show you how to break the body into sections. This will help you draw more realistic poses.

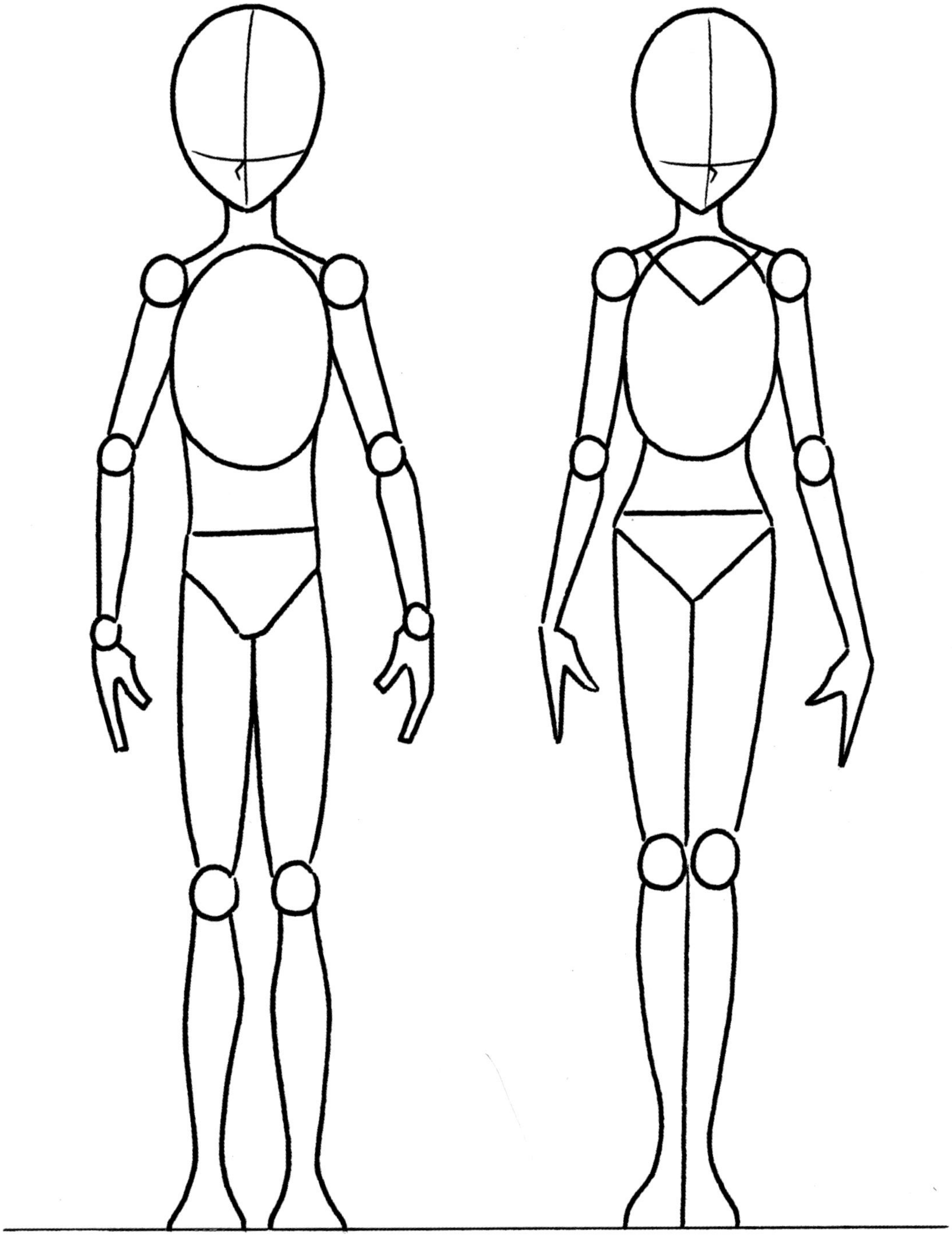

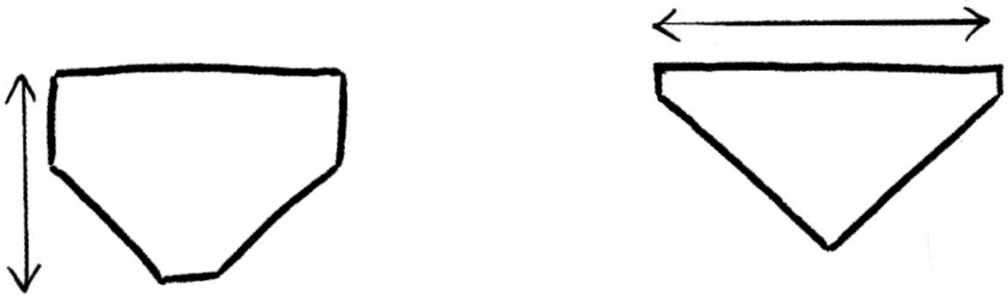

The big difference between the male and female forms is in the hips. Male hips are narrow and tall. Female hips are wide and short.

Basic Poses

Take a paper and pencil, and try sketching some of the poses on this page. *Sketching* means drawing quickly, without worrying about the details. Just try to capture the feeling of each pose. This is great practice for drawing the cool manga characters coming up in just a few pages!

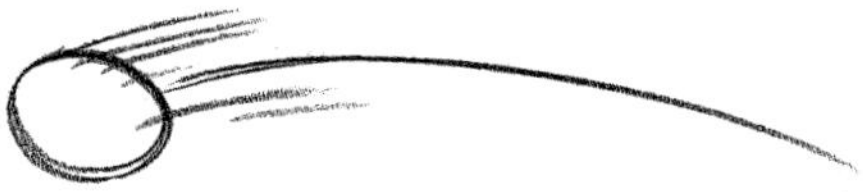

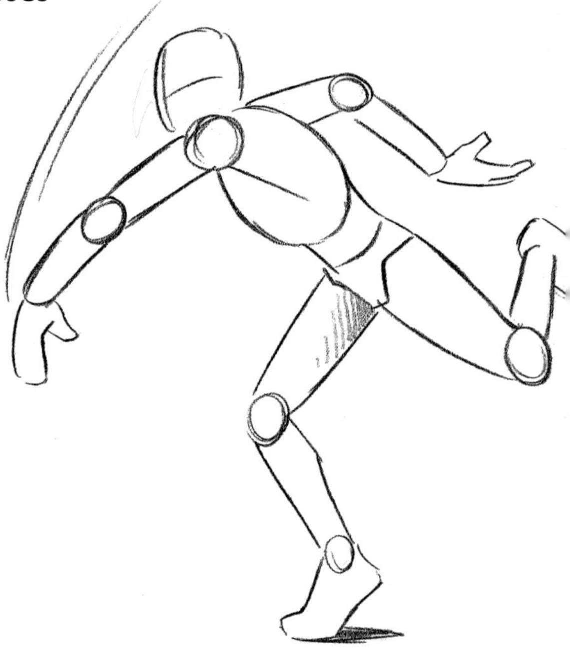

THROWING

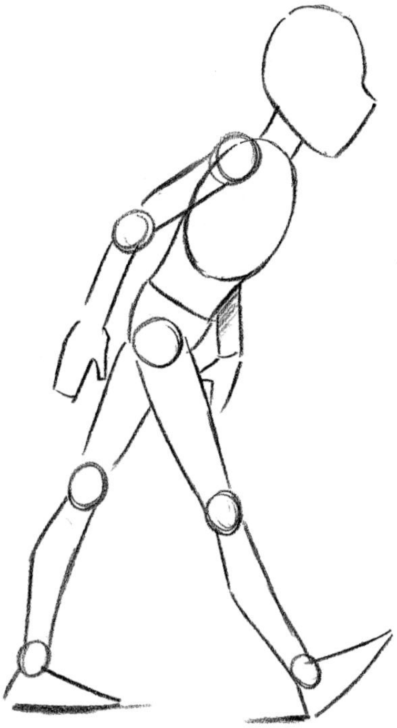

WALKING

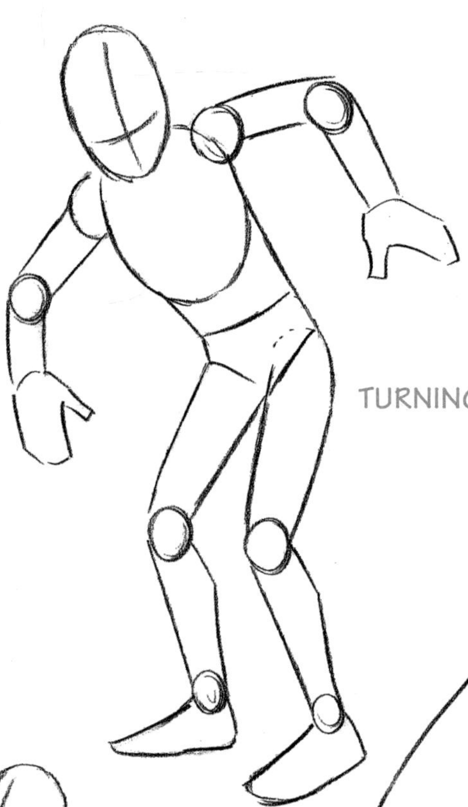

TURNING

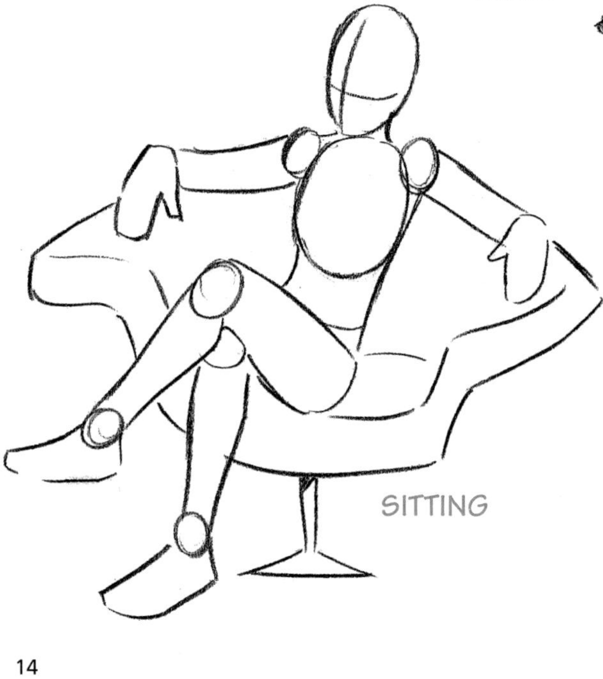

SITTING

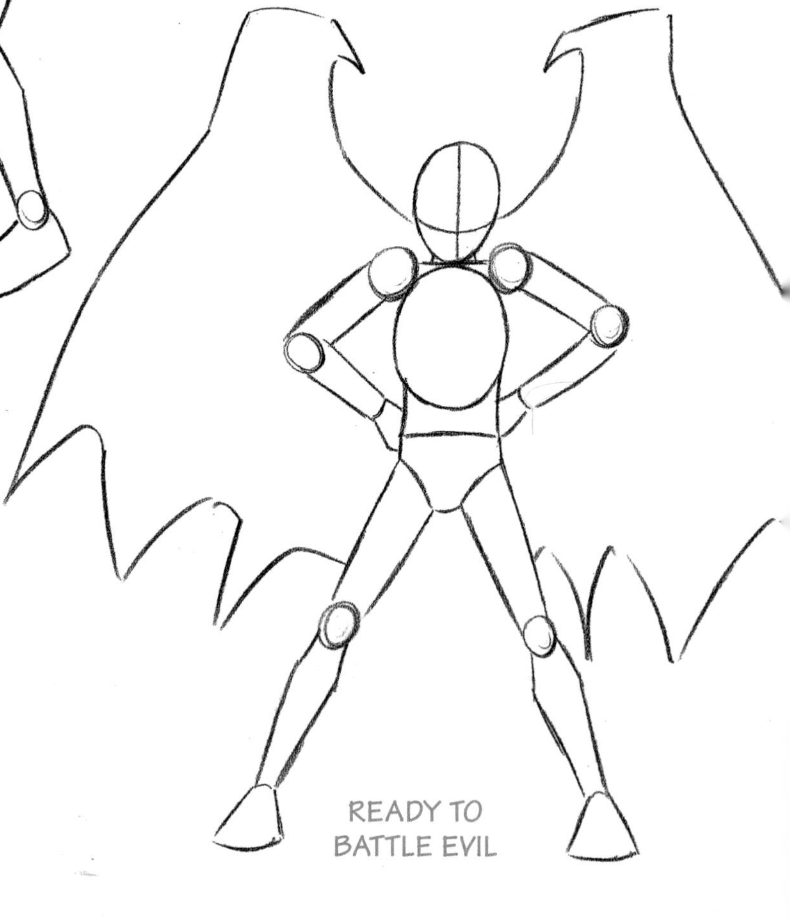

READY TO BATTLE EVIL

More Tips and Tricks

Here are some things to remember that will help you avoid lots of beginner's mistakes.

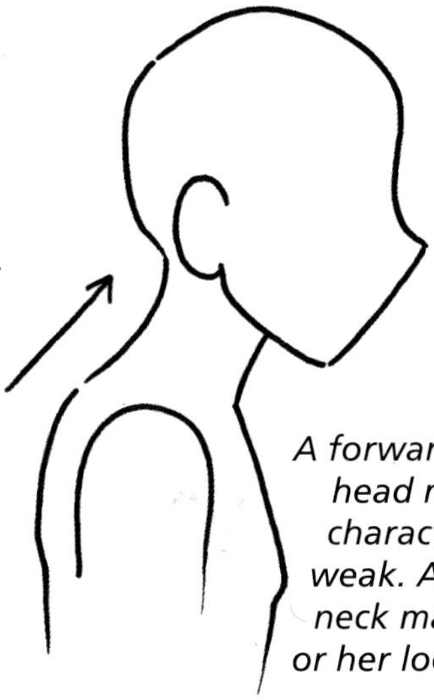

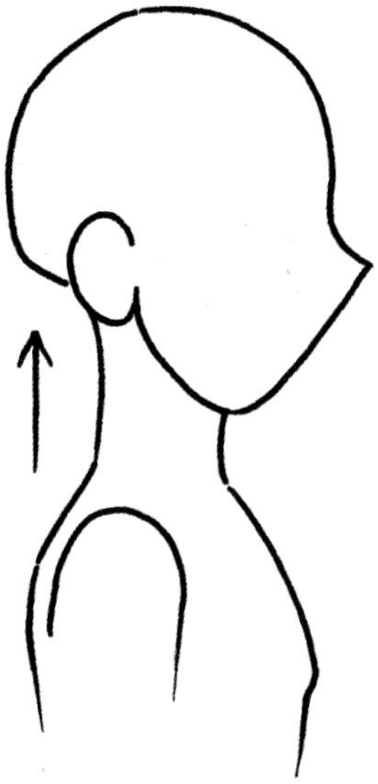

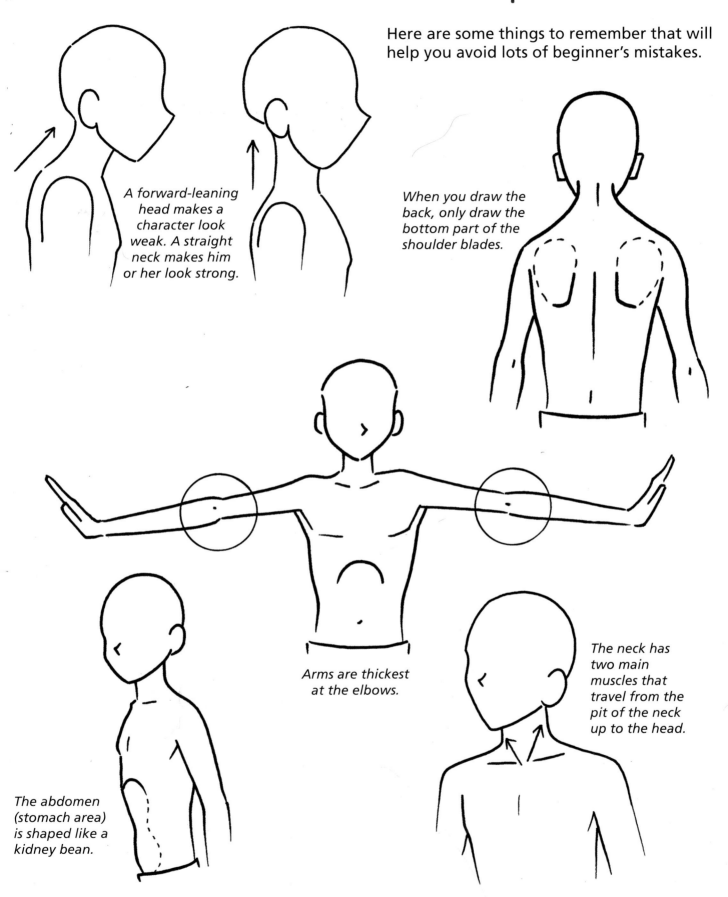

A forward-leaning head makes a character look weak. A straight neck makes him or her look strong.

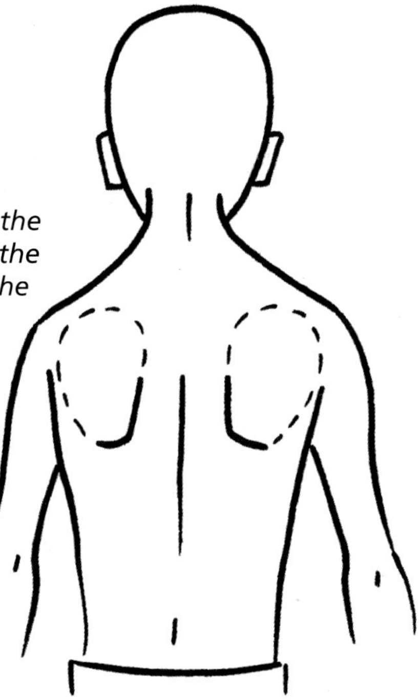

When you draw the back, only draw the bottom part of the shoulder blades.

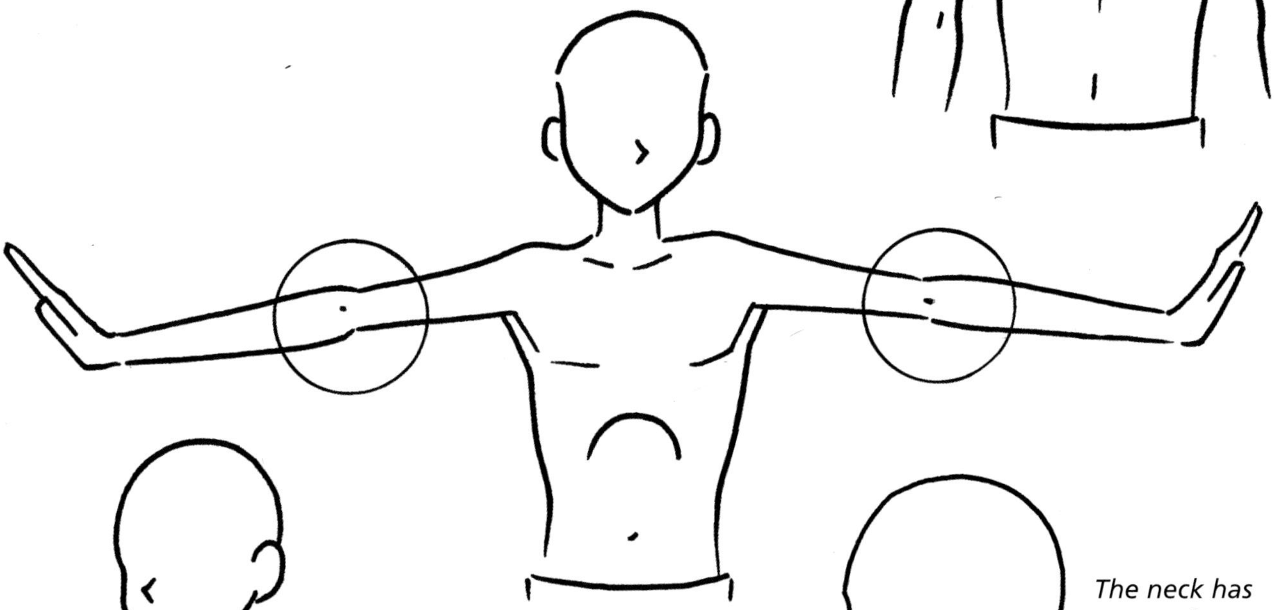

Arms are thickest at the elbows.

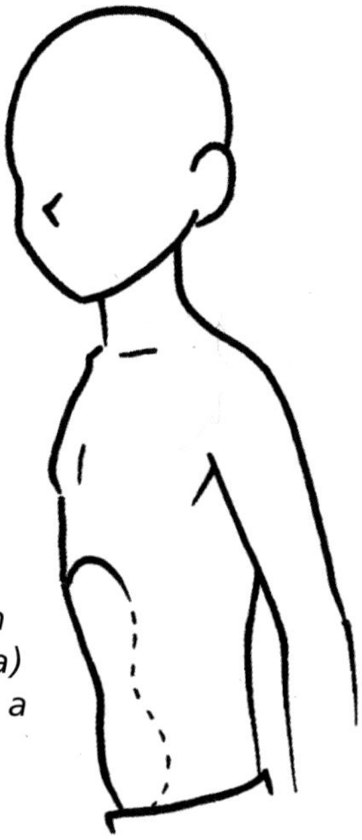

The abdomen (stomach area) is shaped like a kidney bean.

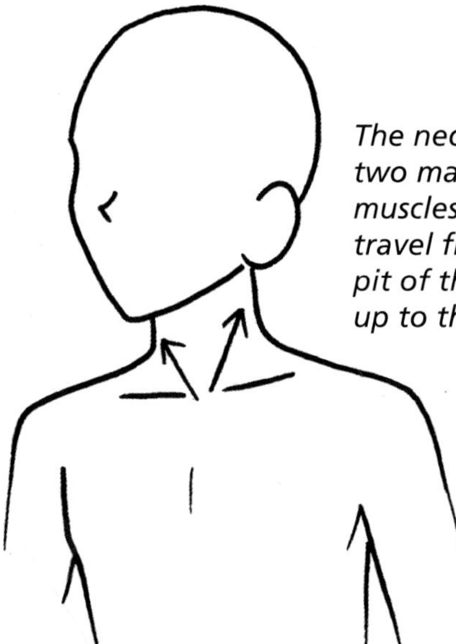

The neck has two main muscles that travel from the pit of the neck up to the head.

Flying Poses

It's fun to watch manga gals and guys zoom through the sky. But if you don't choose just the right position, it can look like your character is falling instead of flying. Here are some sure-fire poses to create a sense of flight. Give 'em a try!

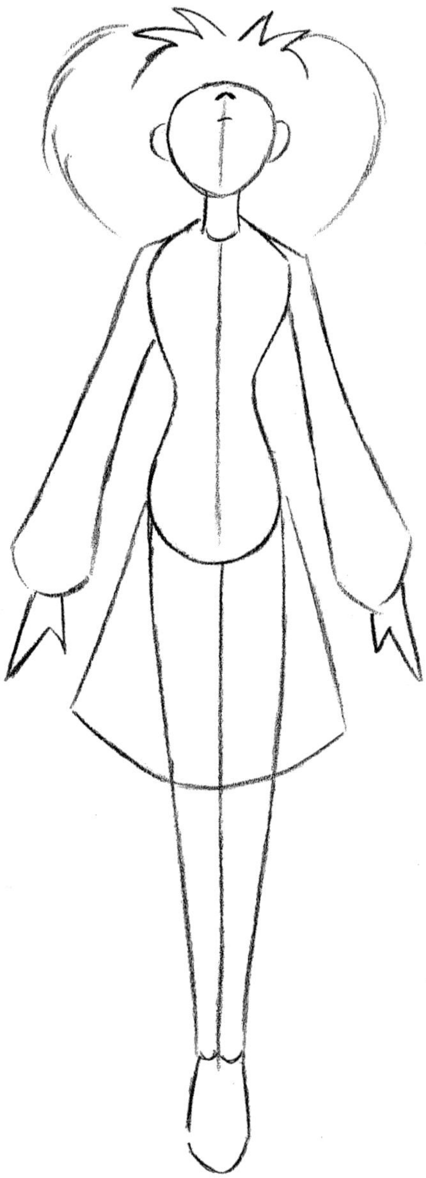

FRONT POSE, ARMS DOWN

This pose only works if the head is tilted up. If she were looking straight at us, it would seem as though she were standing still instead of flying.

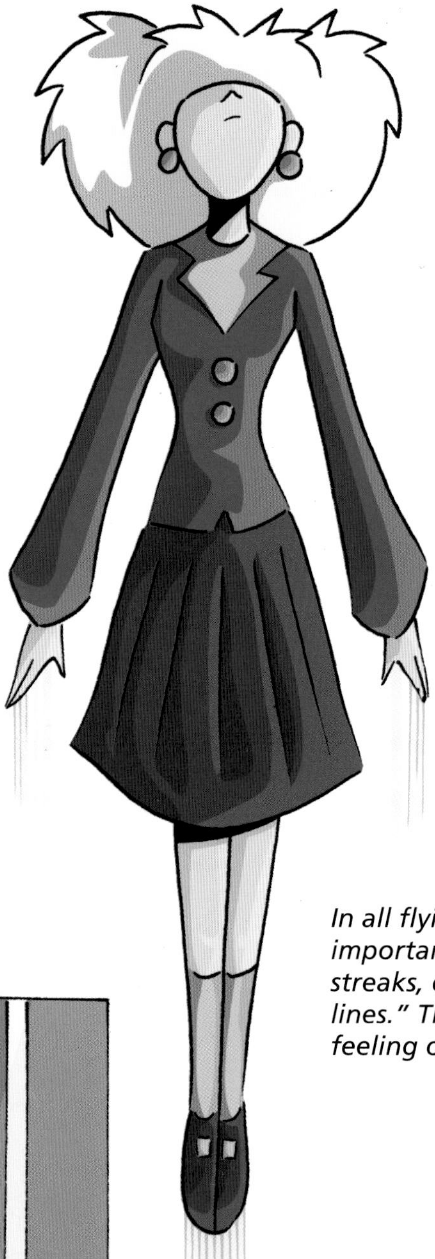

In all flying poses, it's important to add little streaks, called "speed lines." They create a feeling of movement.

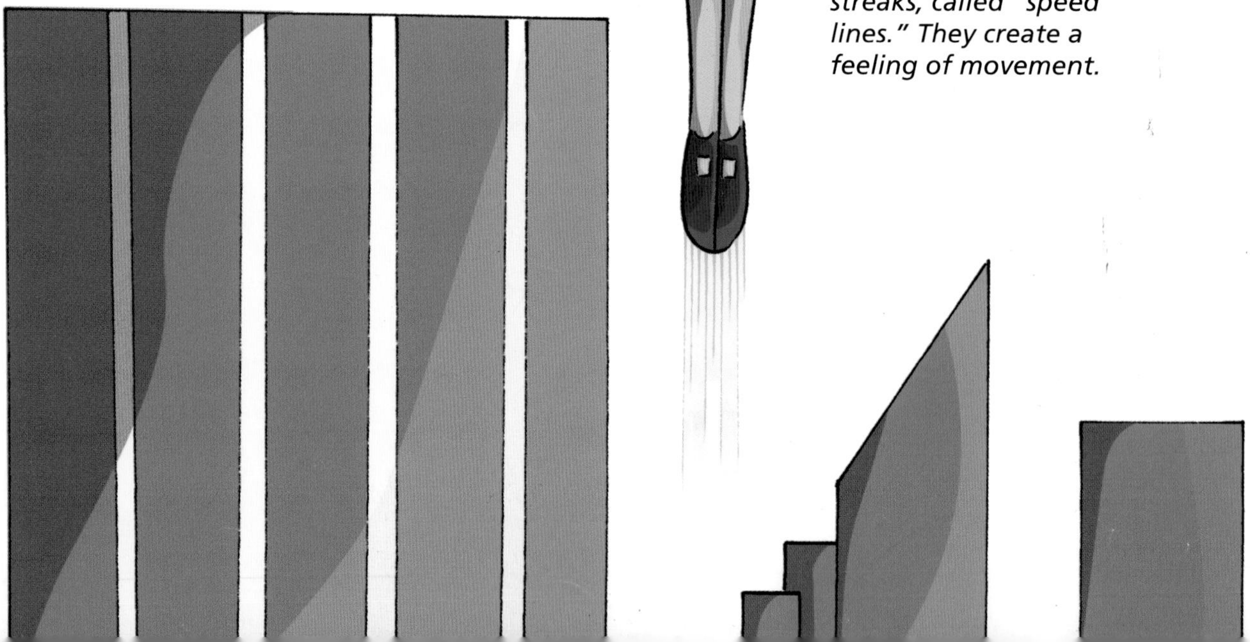

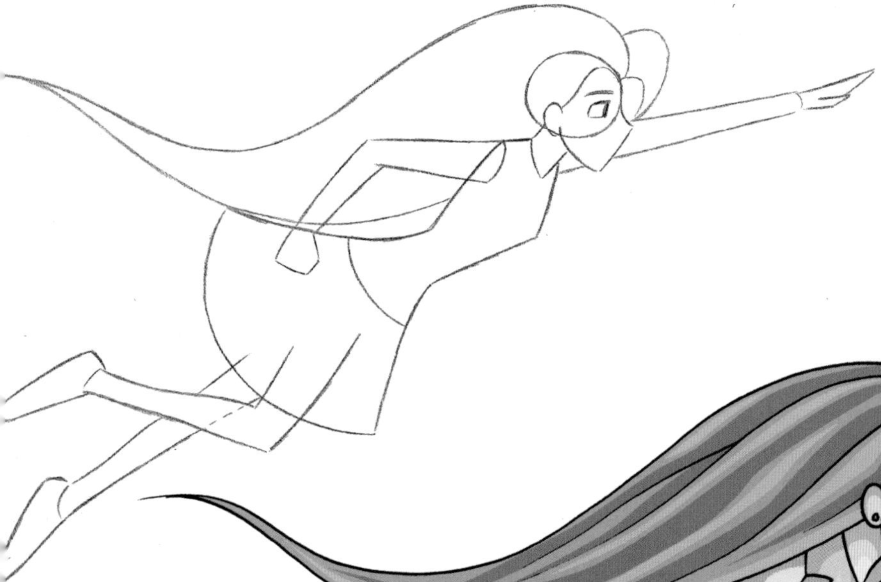

SIDE POSE, ONE ARM FORWARD

Place one arm stretched out straight in front of the character and the other arm back. This is a classic flying pose. Make sure the hair looks like it's being blown by the wind.

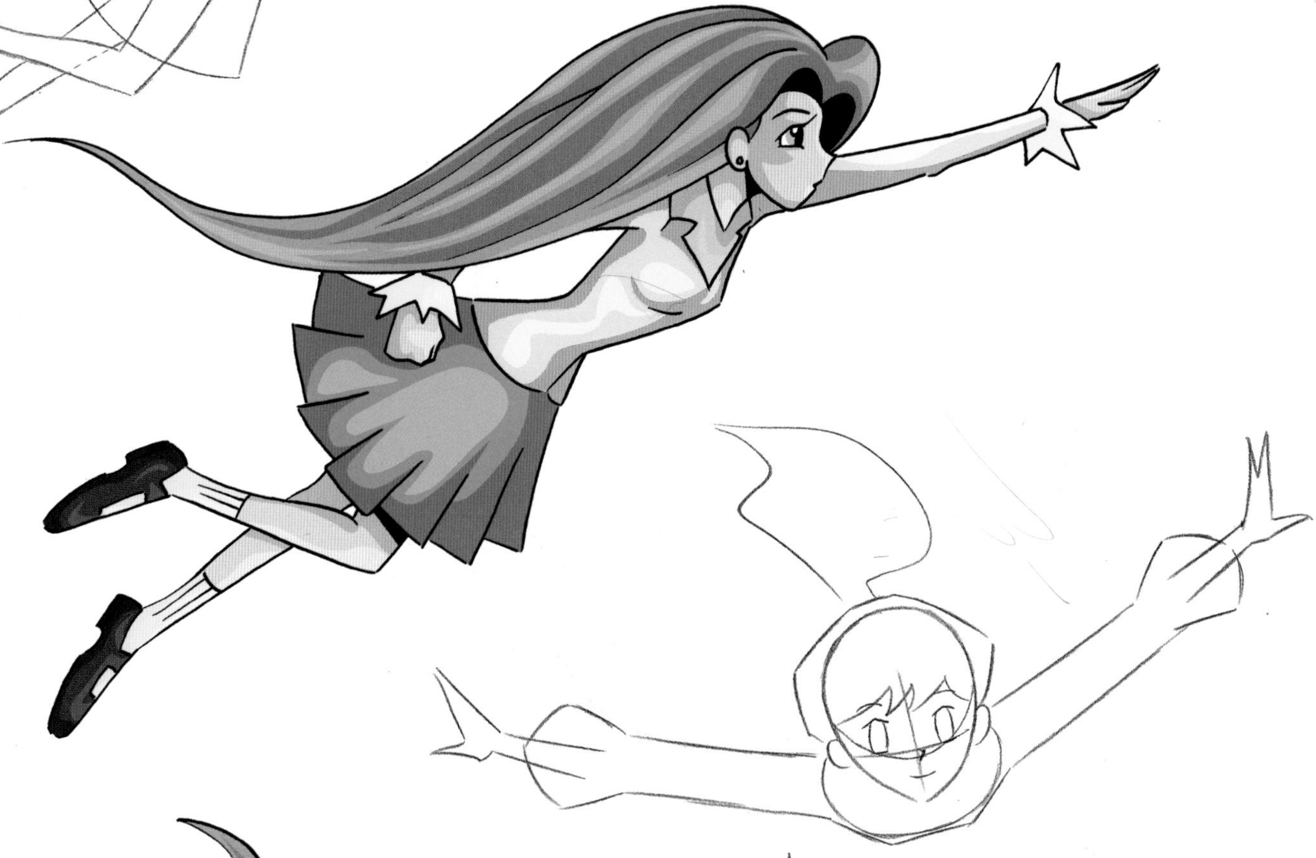

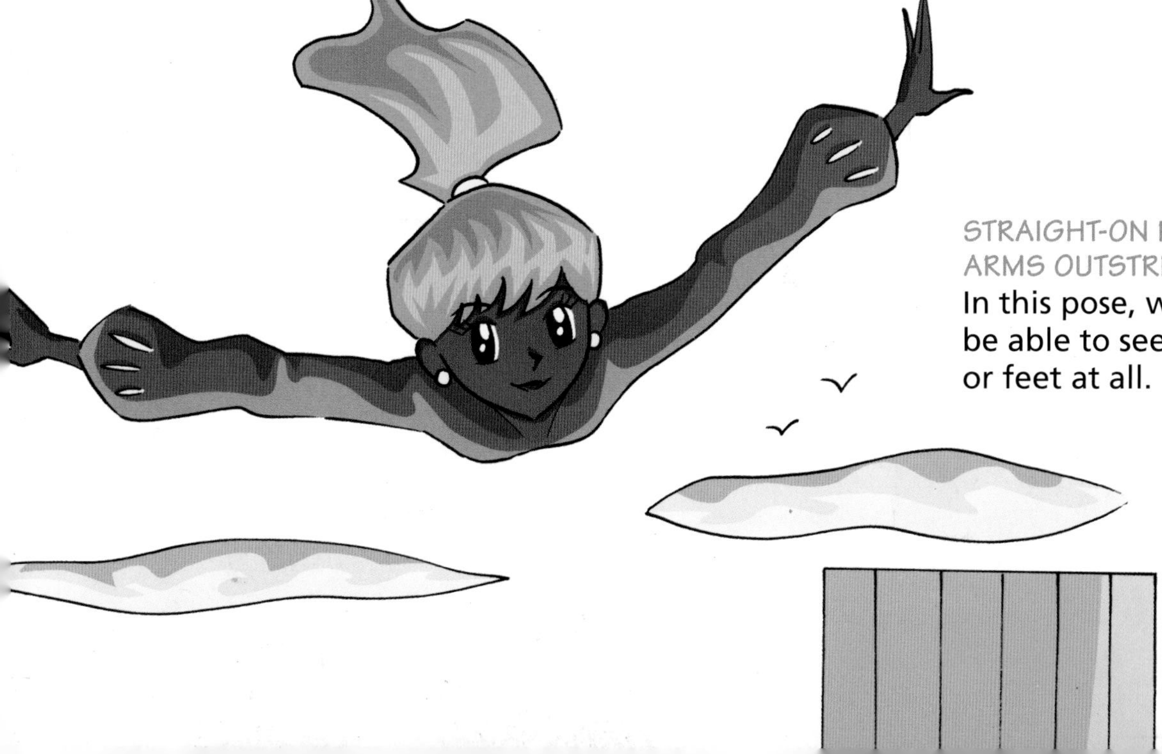

STRAIGHT-ON POSE, ARMS OUTSTRETCHED

In this pose, we shouldn't be able to see the legs or feet at all.

Punching Pose

Whenever one person punches another person, both figures must move in the same direction. It's as important to show the reaction to the punch as it is to show the punch itself!

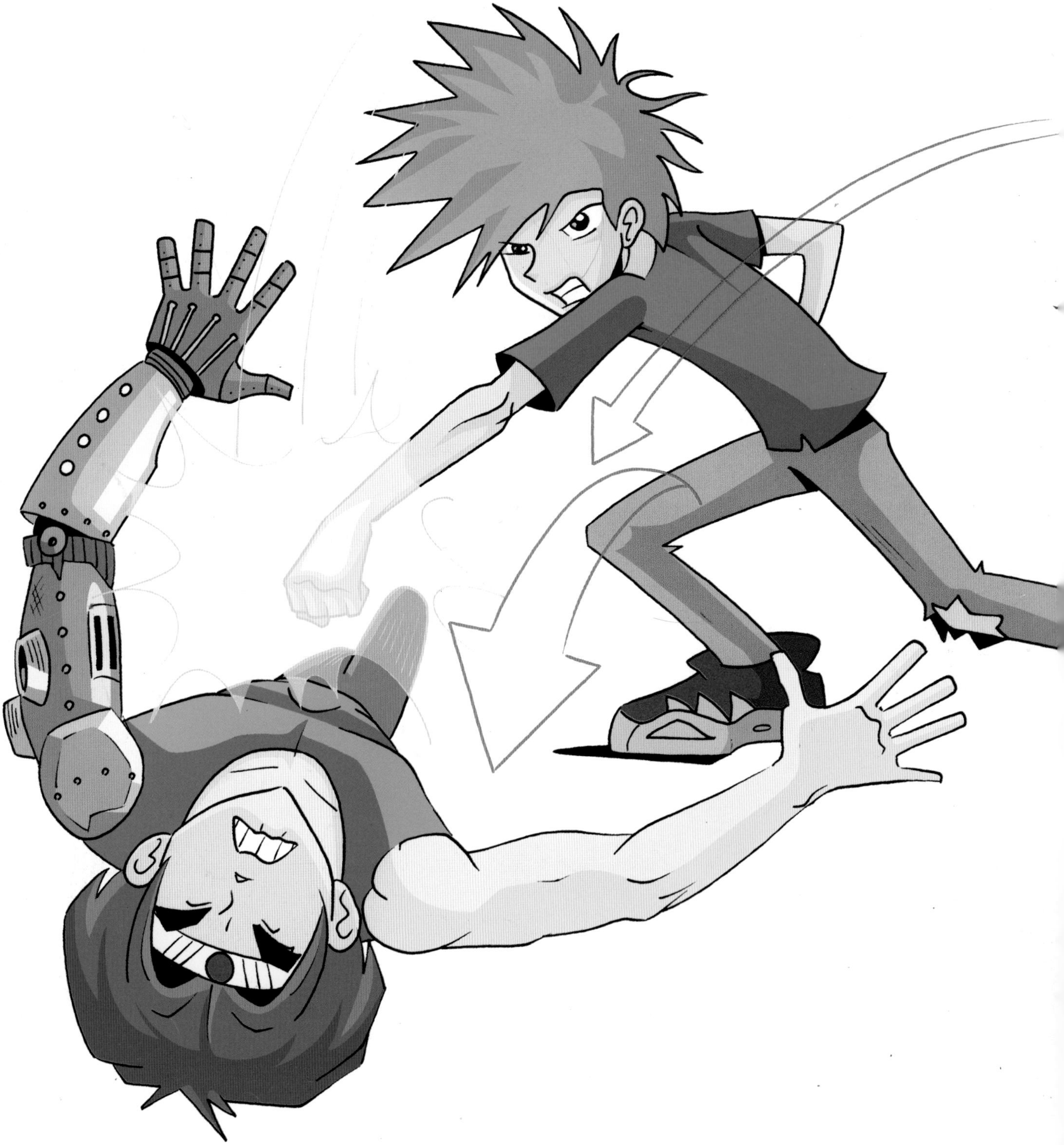

Kicking Pose

Just as with the punch, both figures should move in the same direction.

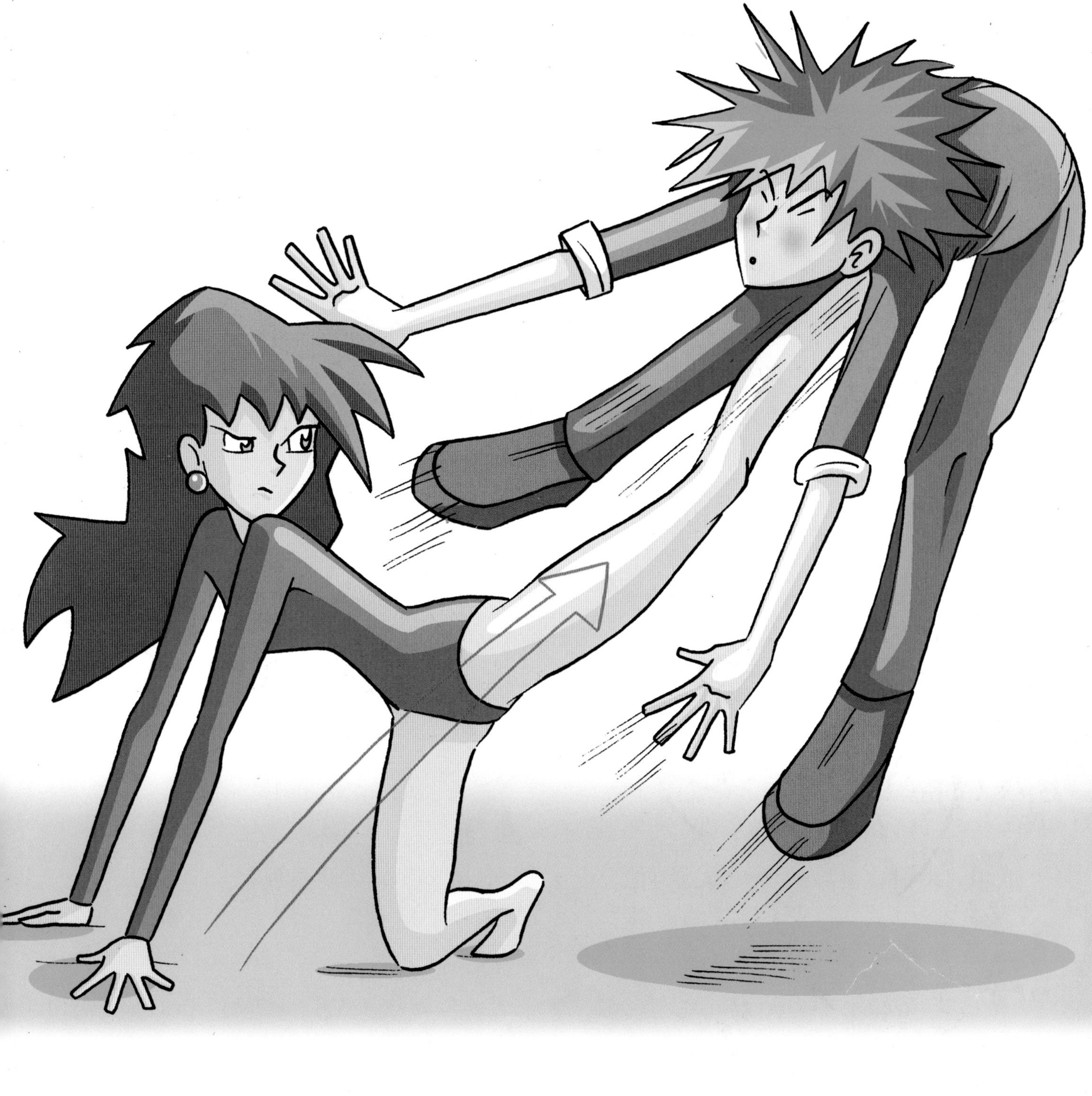

COOL MANGA CHARACTERS

inally, the part you've been waiting for! Now that you've learned the basics, it's time to draw a ton of cool, original manga characters!

Basic Manga Boy

Like all manga characters, this boy has a wide face and a pointy chin.

1. Start with a circle for the top of the head. It's easier to build onto a simple shape than to draw the entire head from scratch.

2. Add the chin.

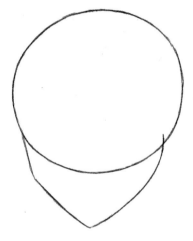

3. Put some guidelines on the face. These are lines that artists use to help them put the features on the face. They also show which way the head is facing.

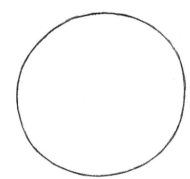

4. Place the facial features on the guidelines. The eyes go on the horizontal guideline. The bridge of the nose goes on the vertical guideline. The mouth is drawn off-center. Make the eyebrows bold. Place the ear where the jaw and the top of the head meet.

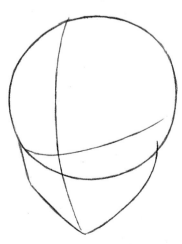

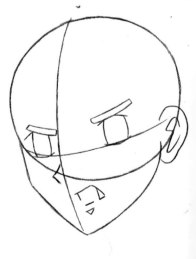

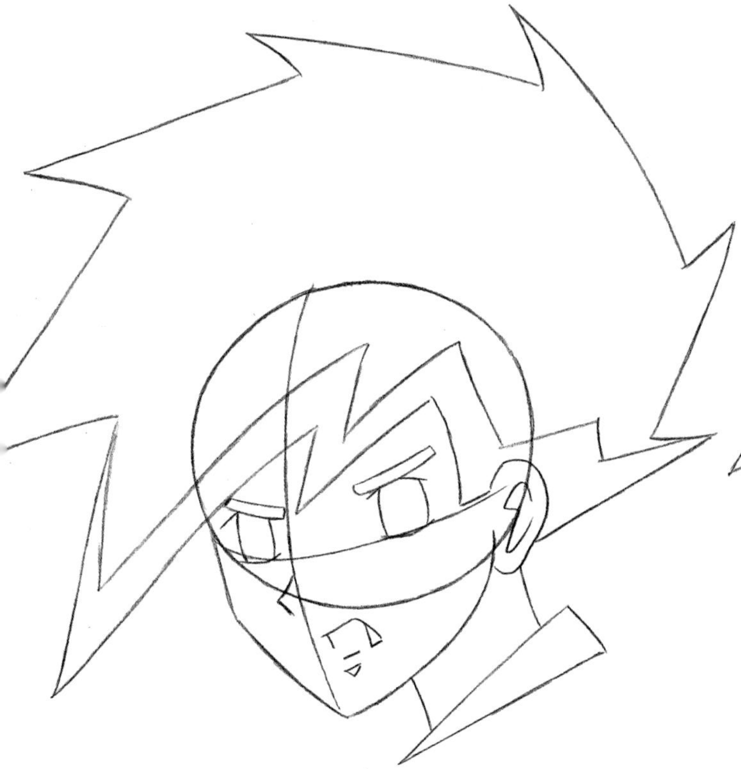

5. Manga characters are famous for their hairstyles—always overdo it! Also, add a neck and collar.

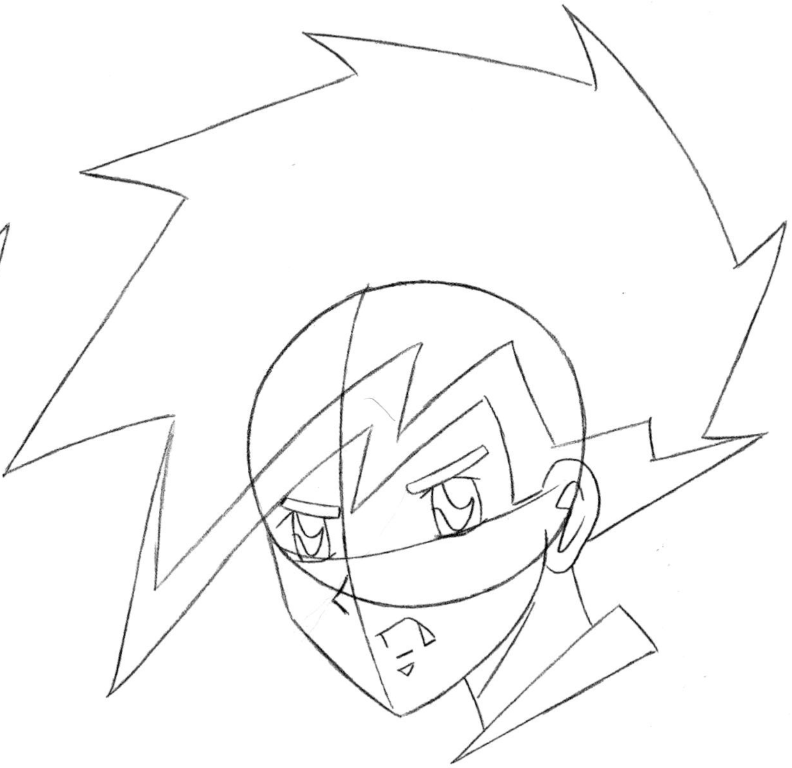

6. Put shines in the eyes. Add a shadow under the chin.

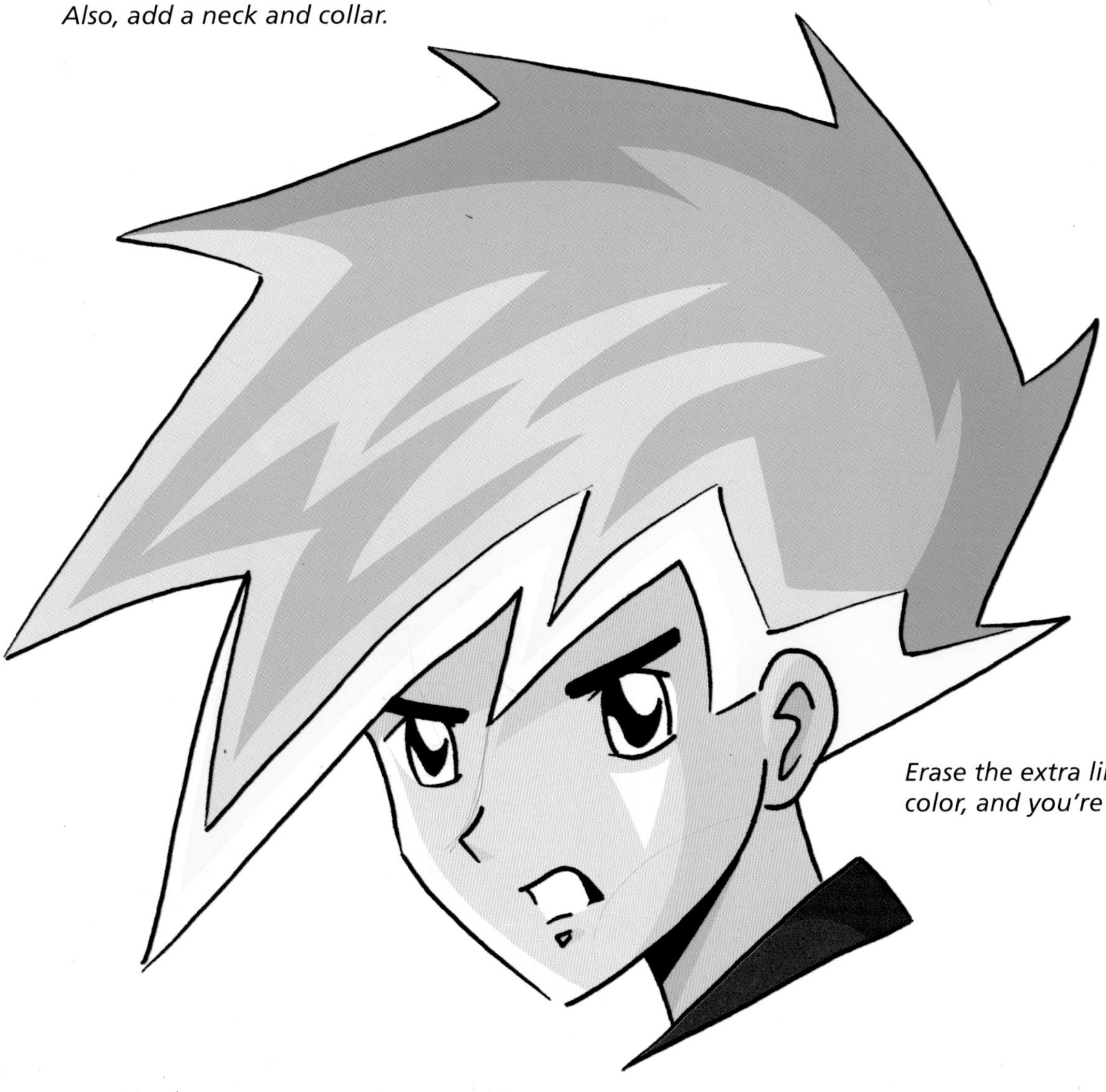

Erase the extra lines, add color, and you're done!

Basic Manga Girl

Now let's do the same basic pose, but for a girl.

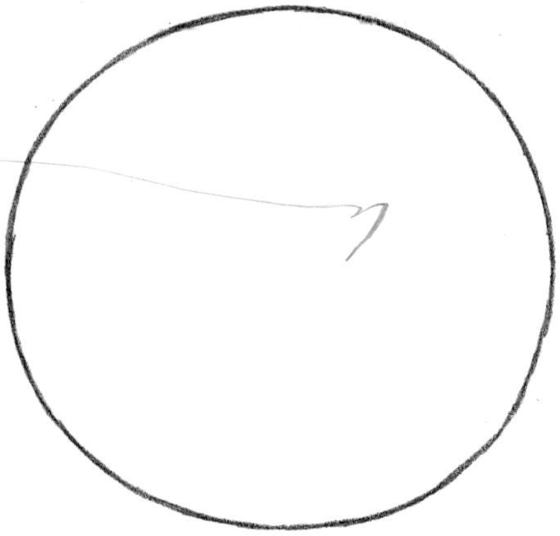

1. Draw a circle for the top of the head.

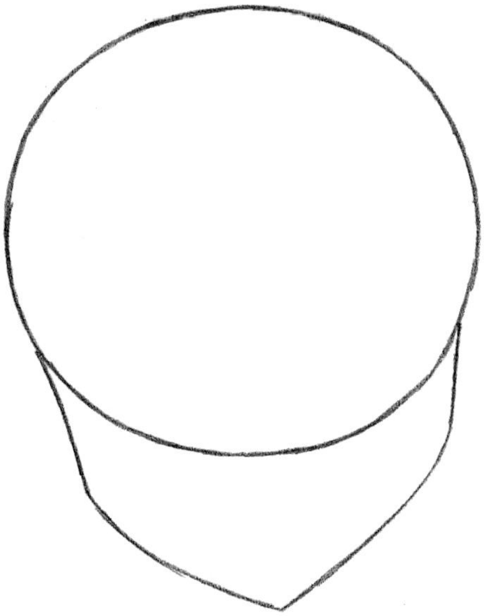

2. Add the chin.

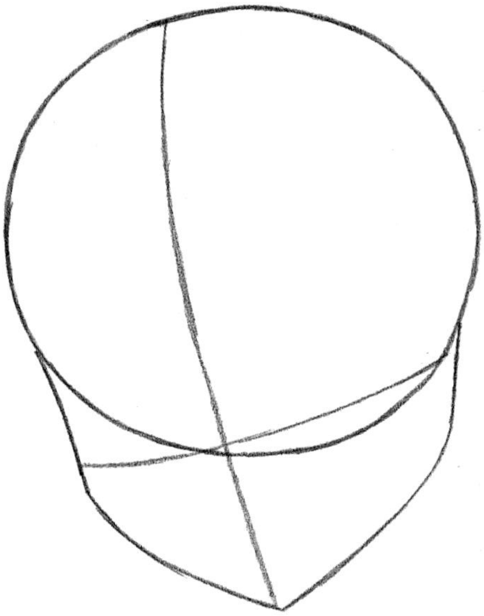

3. Draw the guidelines.

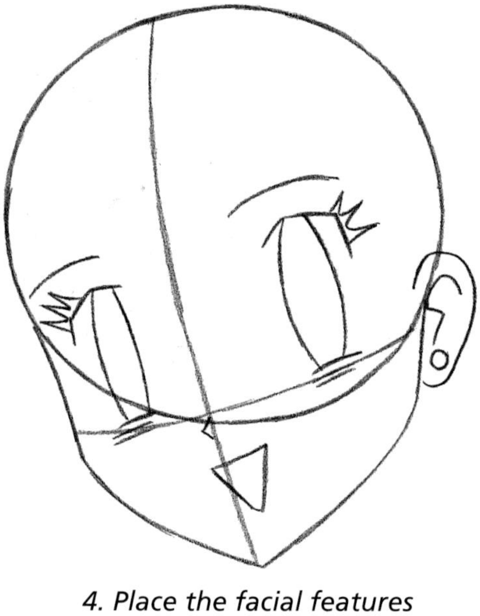

4. Place the facial features on the guidelines.

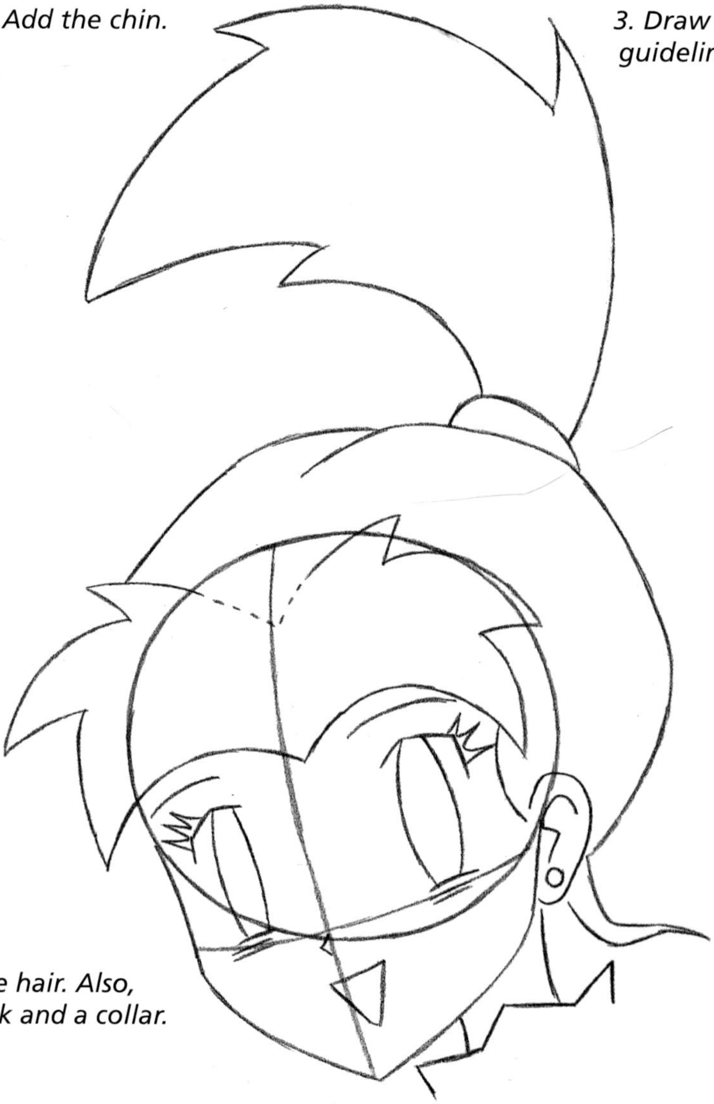

5. Add the hair. Also, add a neck and a collar.

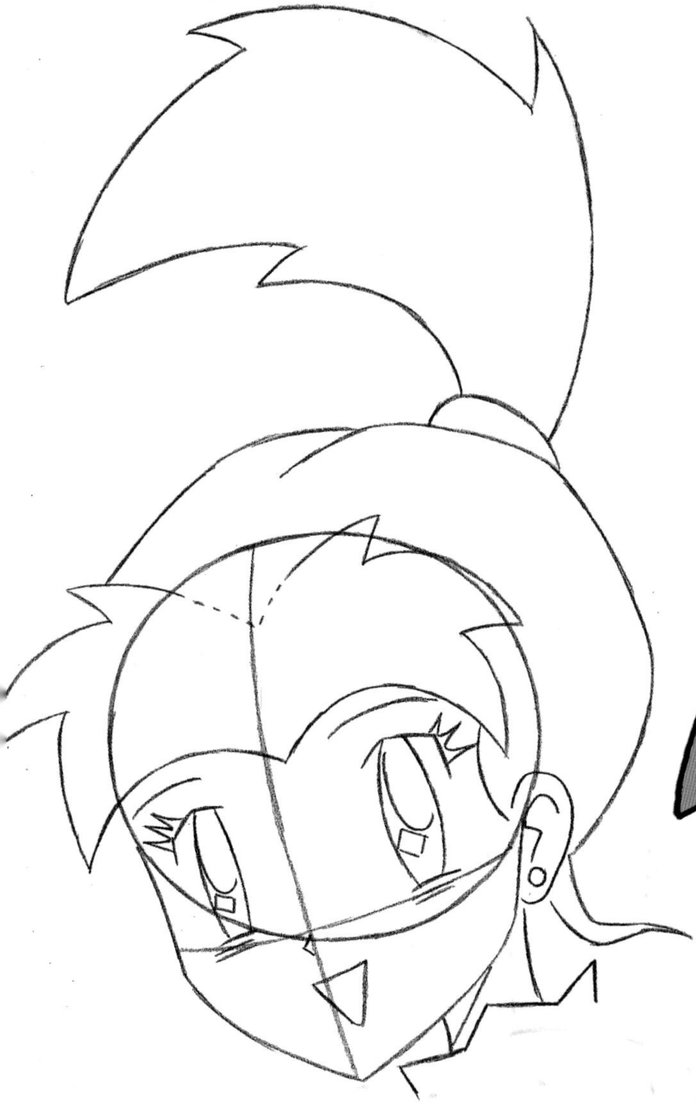

6. Put shines in the eyes. Add a shadow just below the chin.

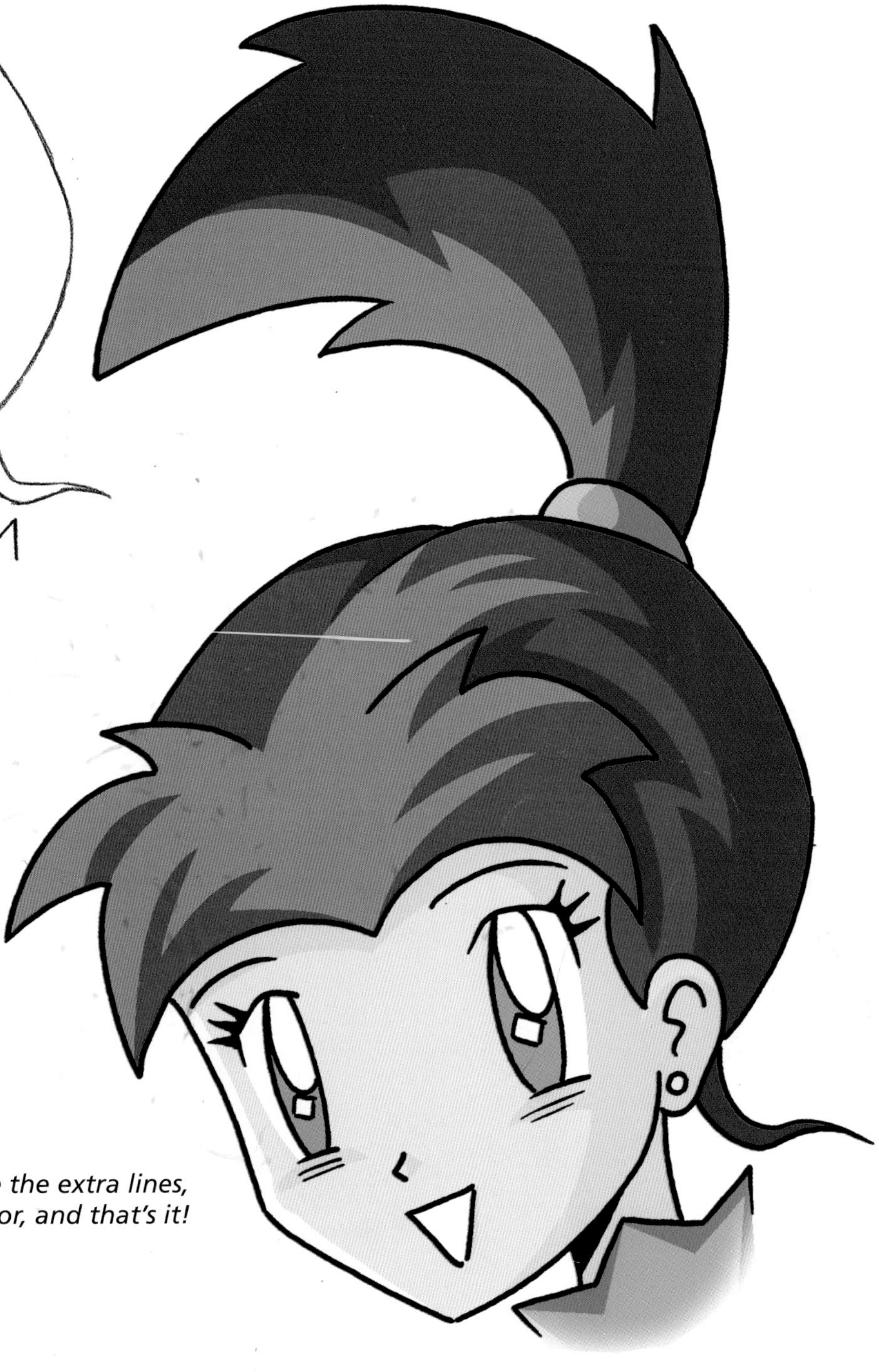

7. Erase the extra lines, add color, and that's it!

Pointy-Haired Guy

Here's another basic manga boy. Since you know the basics by now, I'll use fewer steps.

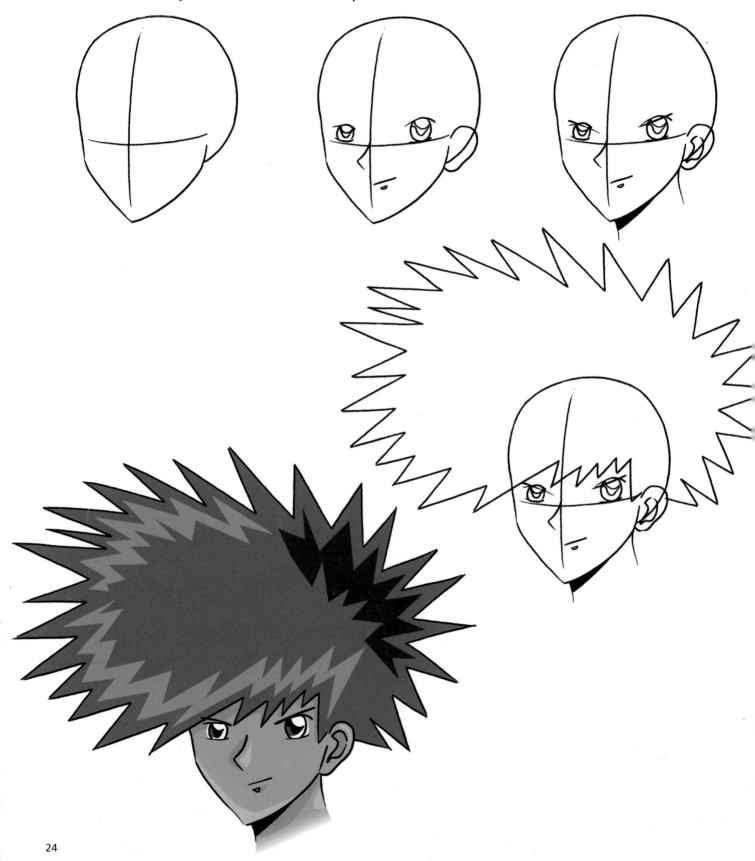

Worried Boy

This character has interesting eyes and a different hairstyle. But notice that he still has the same basic manga style: big head and pointy chin.

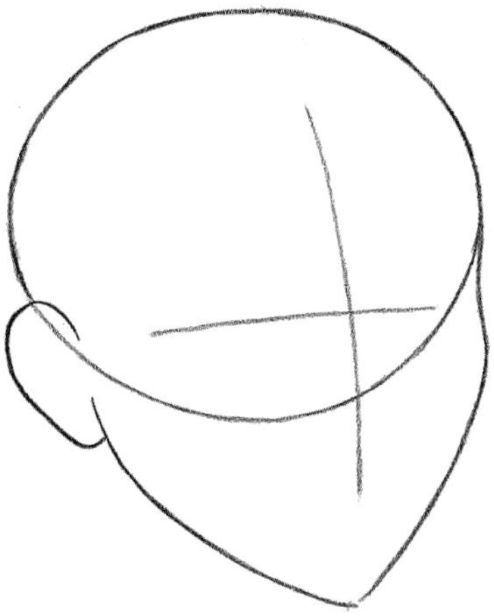

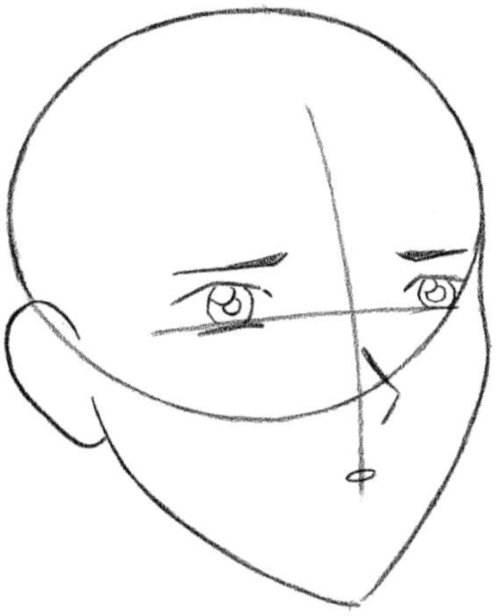

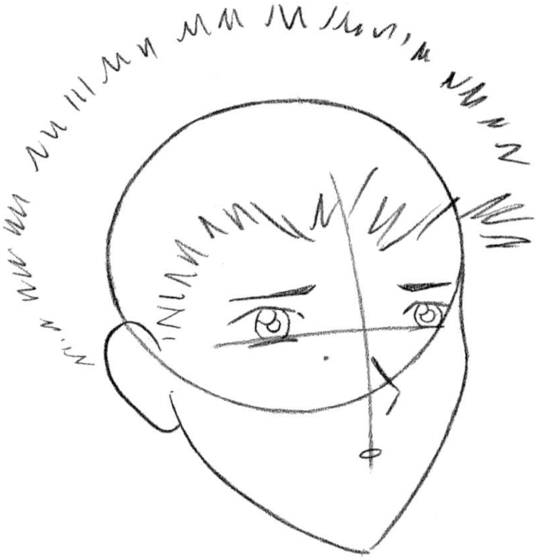

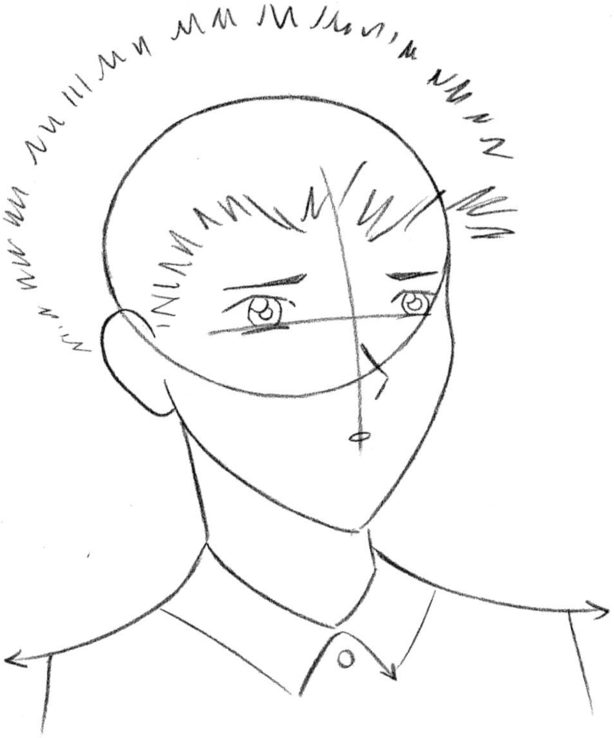

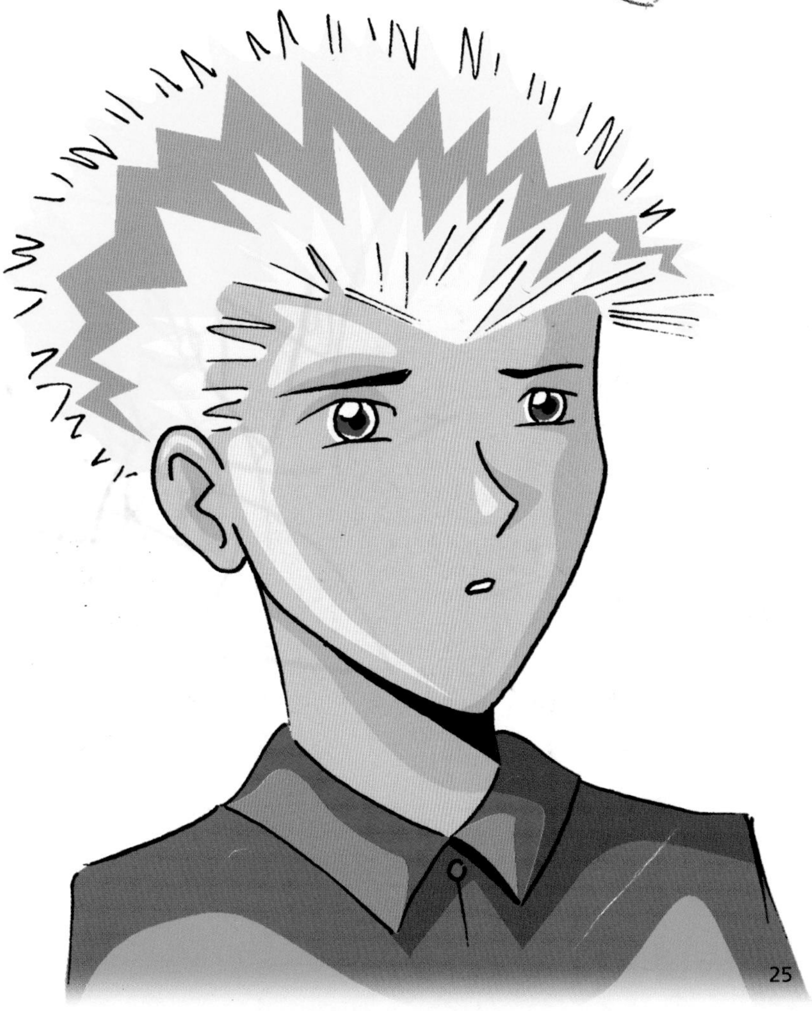

Schoolgirl

Here's a figure for you to try. As with all drawings, concentrate on the big shapes first and save the details for last.

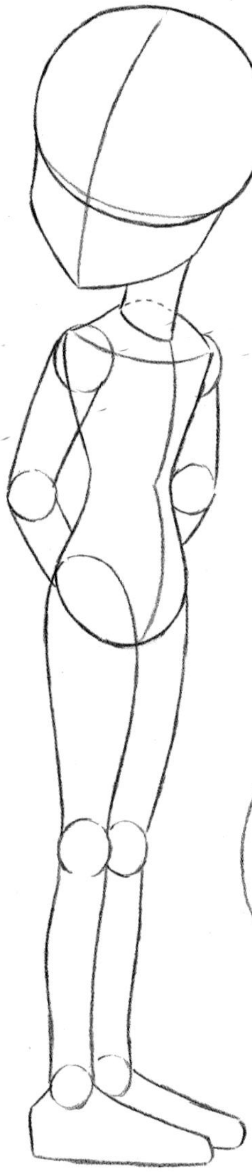

1. Start by building the body with basic shapes.

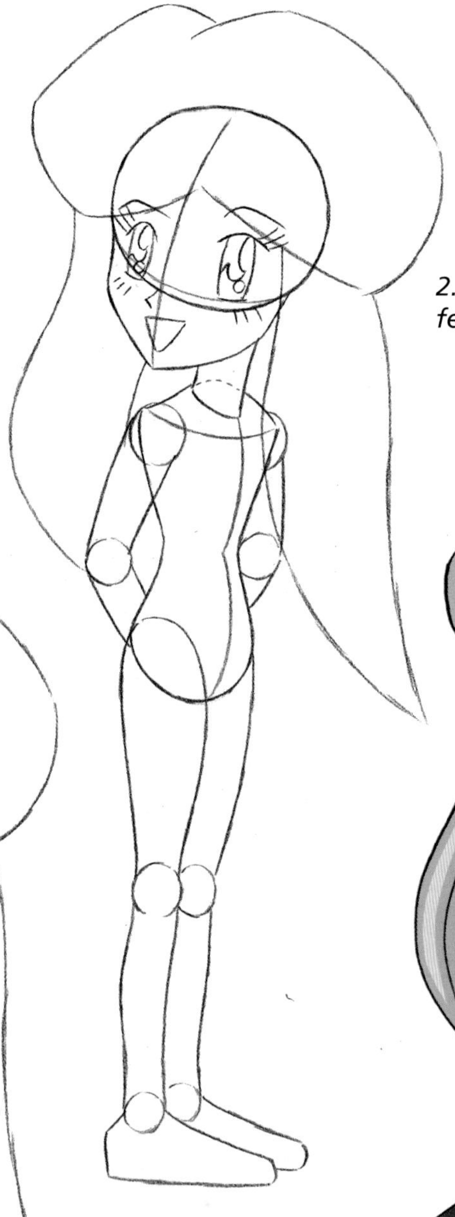

2. Add the facial features and hair.

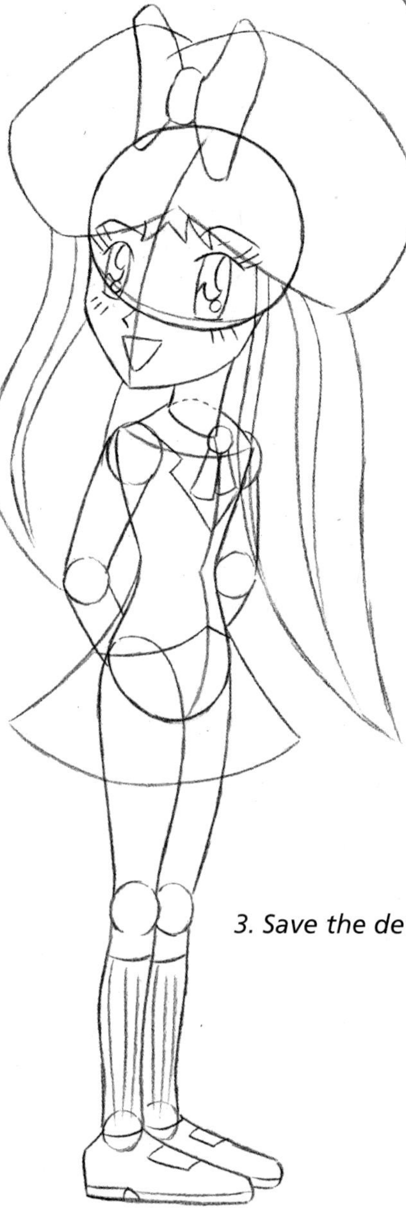

3. Save the details for last!

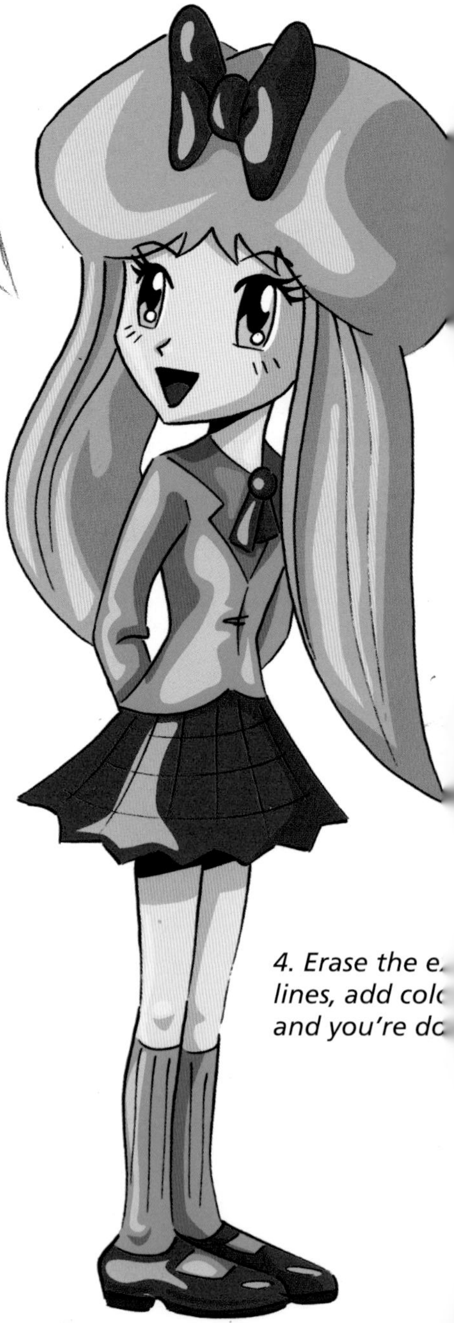

4. Erase the e
lines, add colo
and you're do

Funny Runner

Most people lean forward when they run. To draw a goofy run, make your character lean back, chest out, with both arms behind. Don't let either foot touch the ground. The shadow below him is a nice touch—it tells people where the ground is.

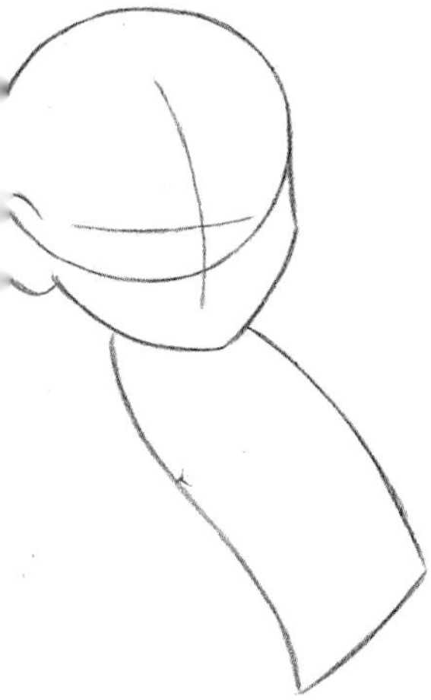

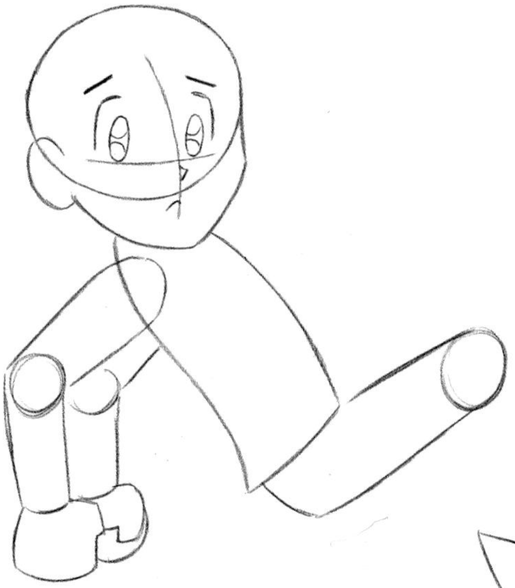

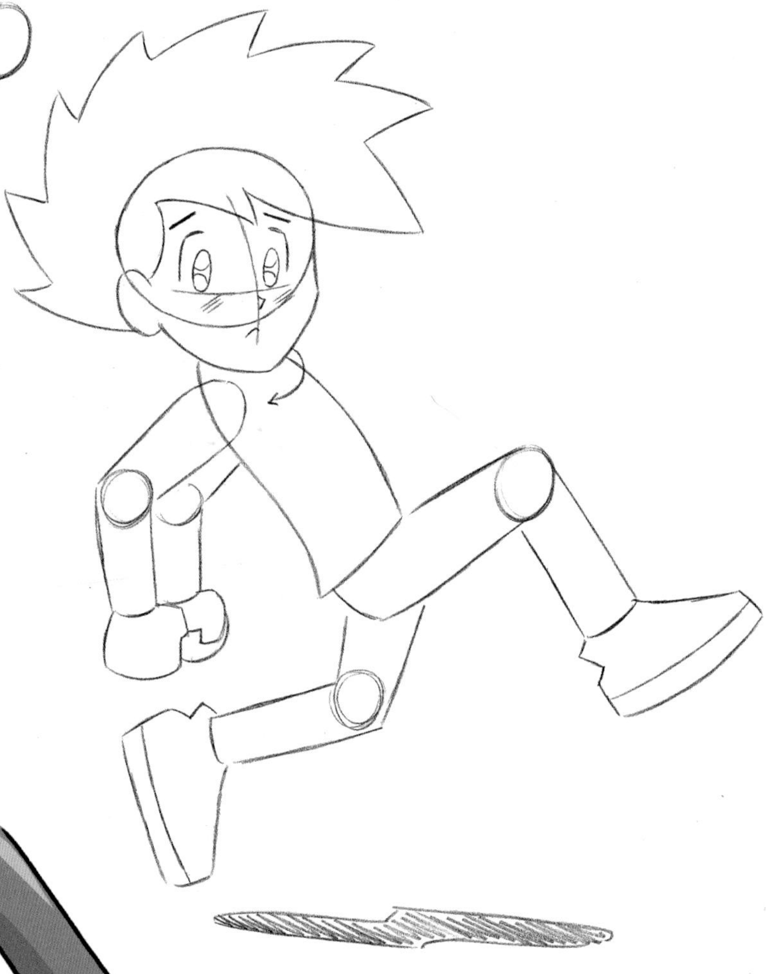

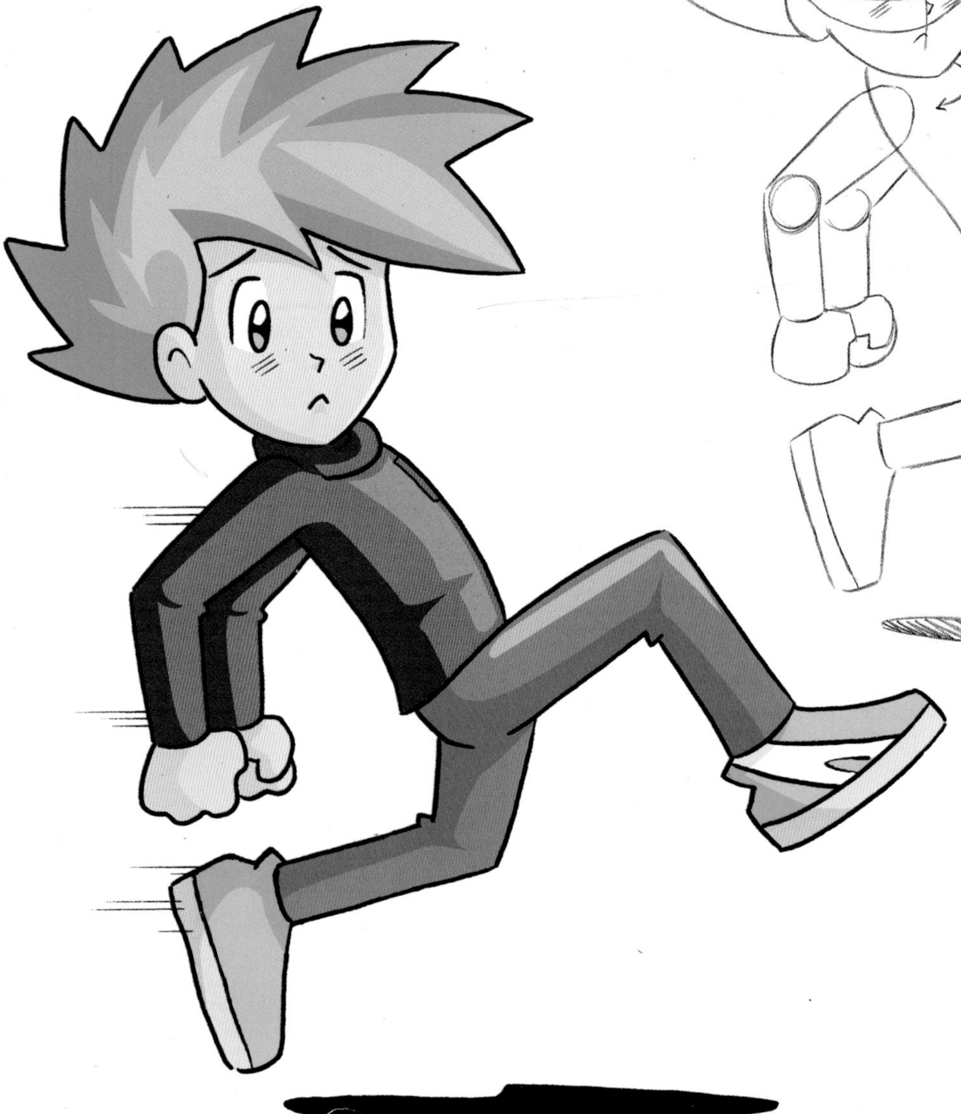

Crabby Cathy

What a grouch! I can easily imagine this girl as somebody's mean older sister. Those upturned braids are prickly reminders of her personality. And her arm position, called "arms akimbo," shows her to be quite demanding.

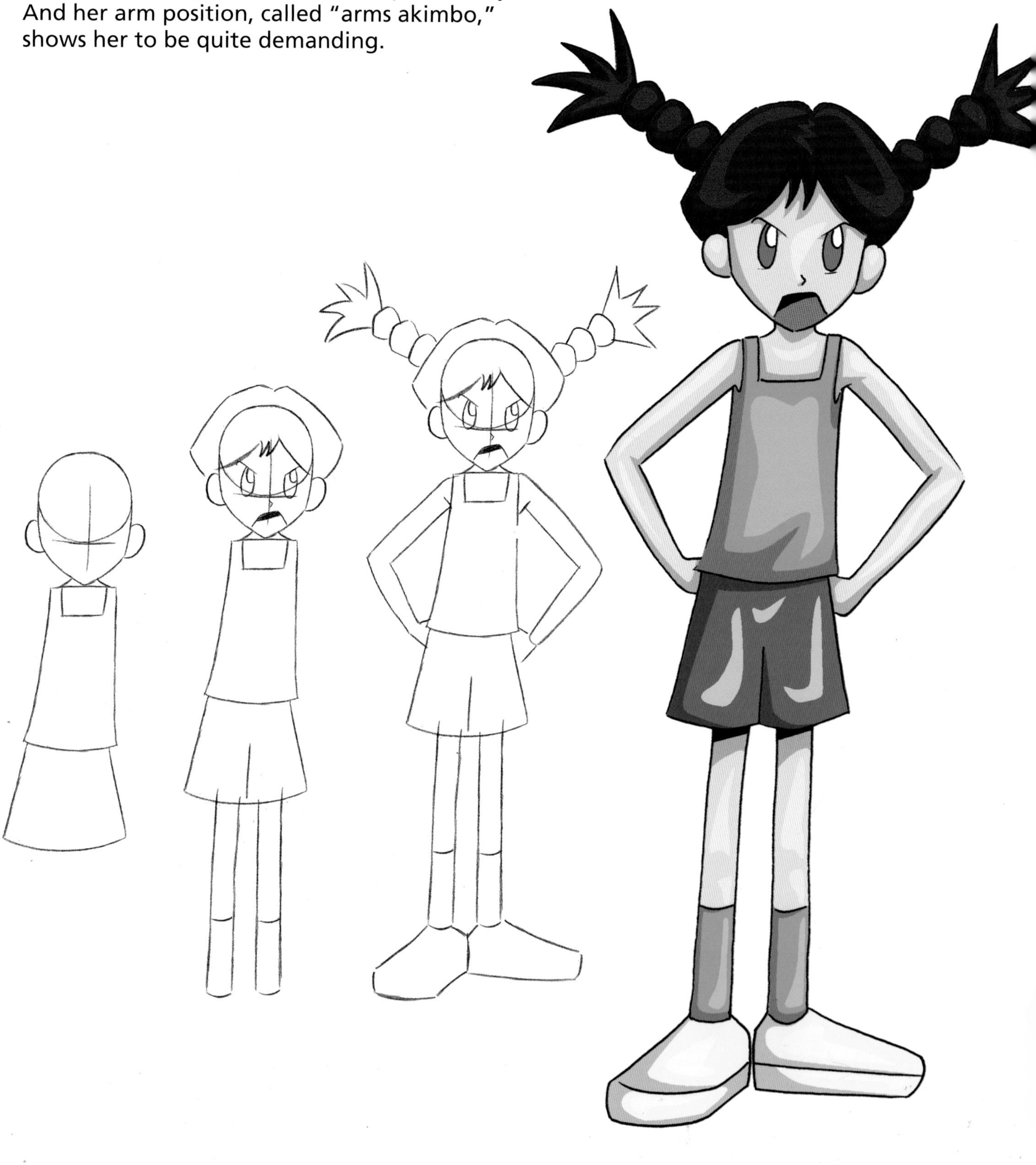

Manga Princess

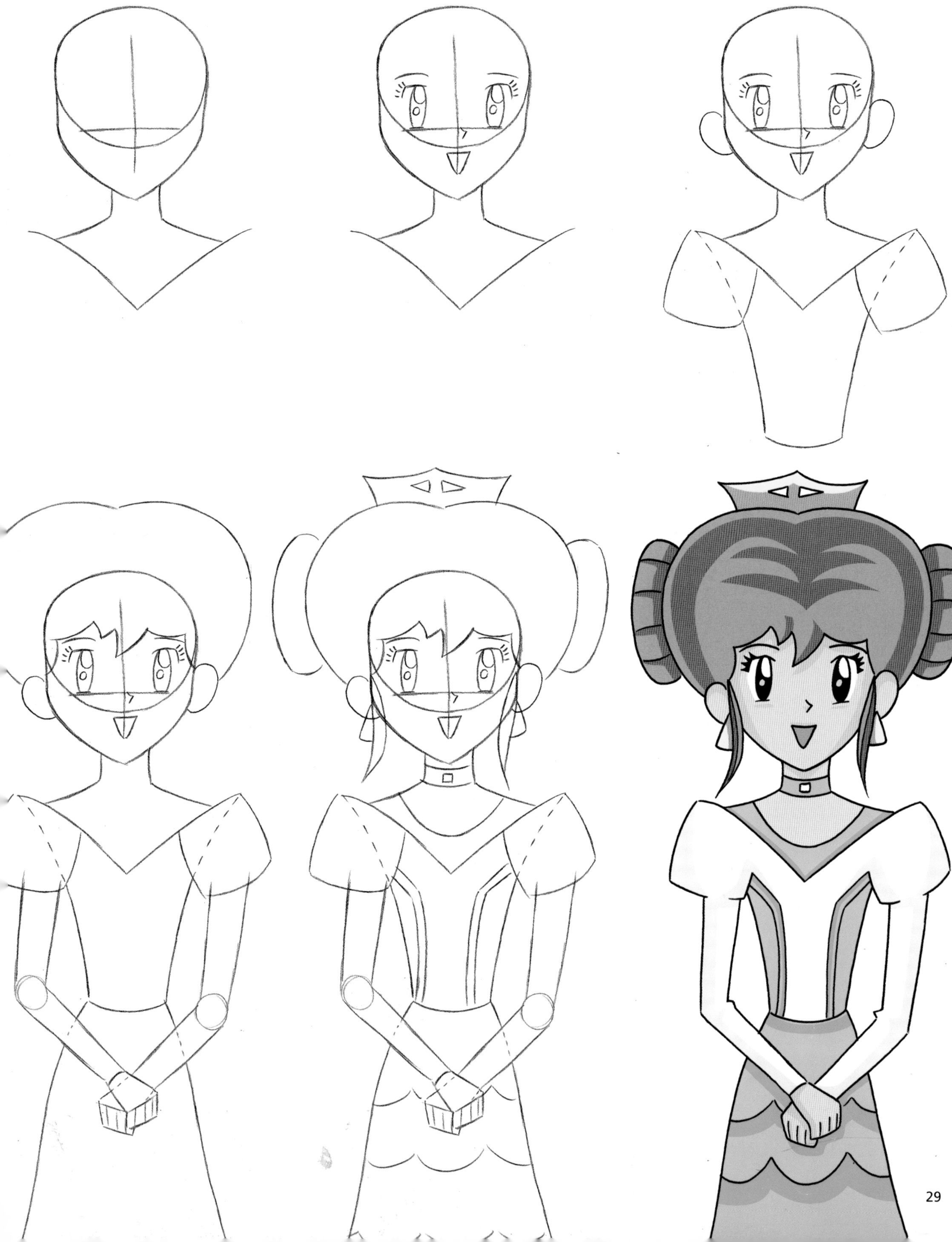

Casual Teen

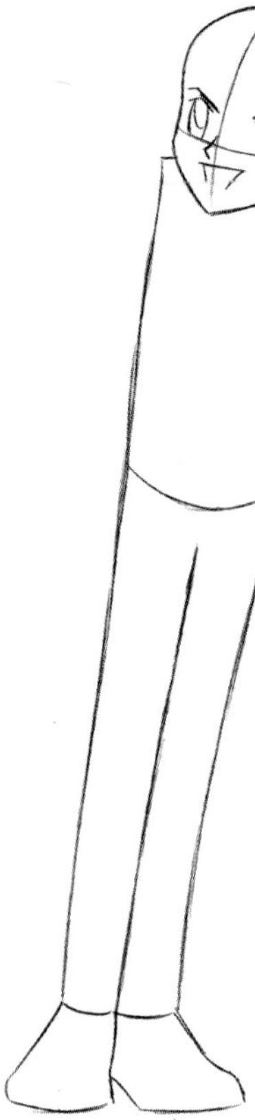

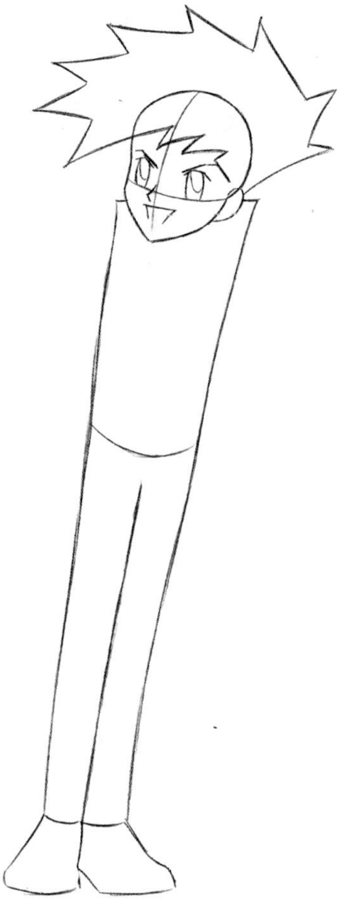

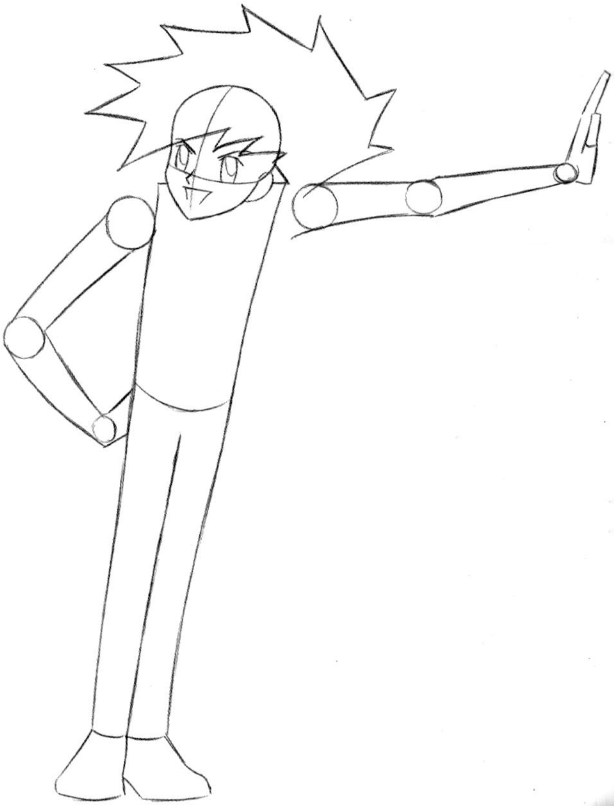

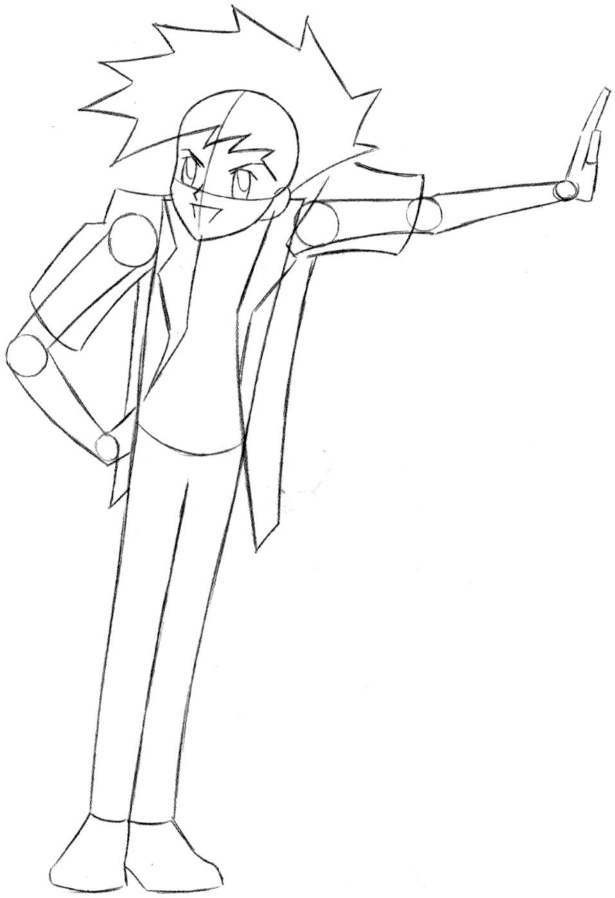

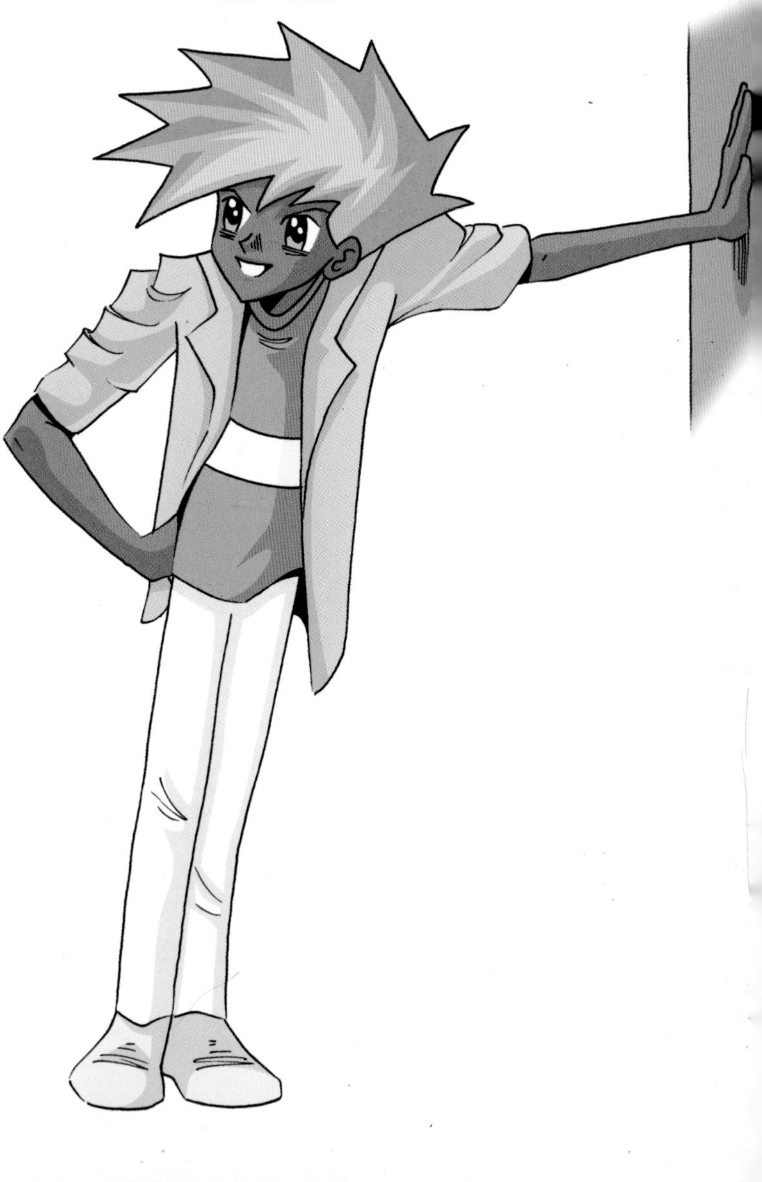

Warrior Princess

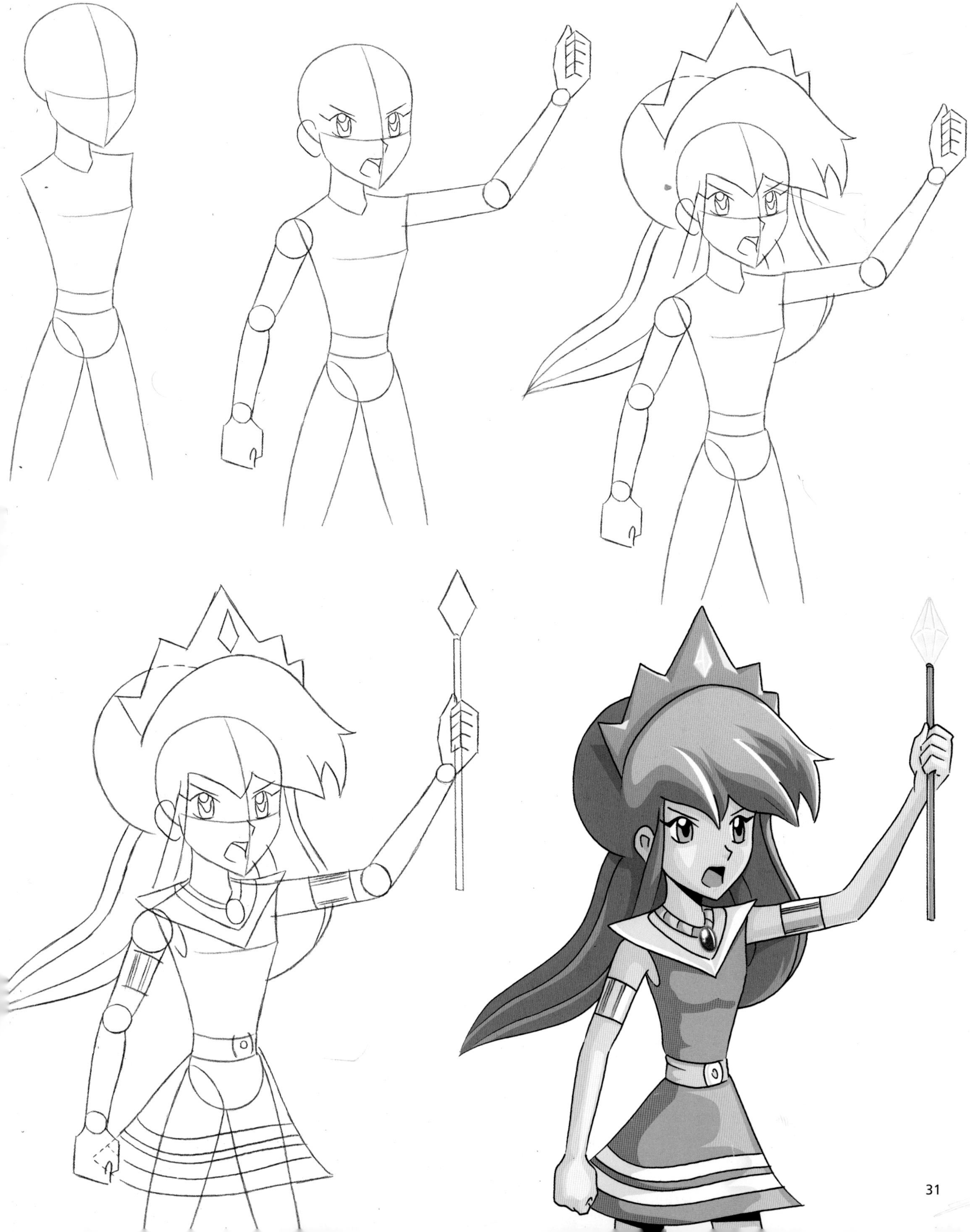

Teenage Defender

Teens play an important role in manga—they save the world! It's hard to do battle with only a candy bar and a baseball glove, so manga artists often give their characters a little help, like this laser blaster.

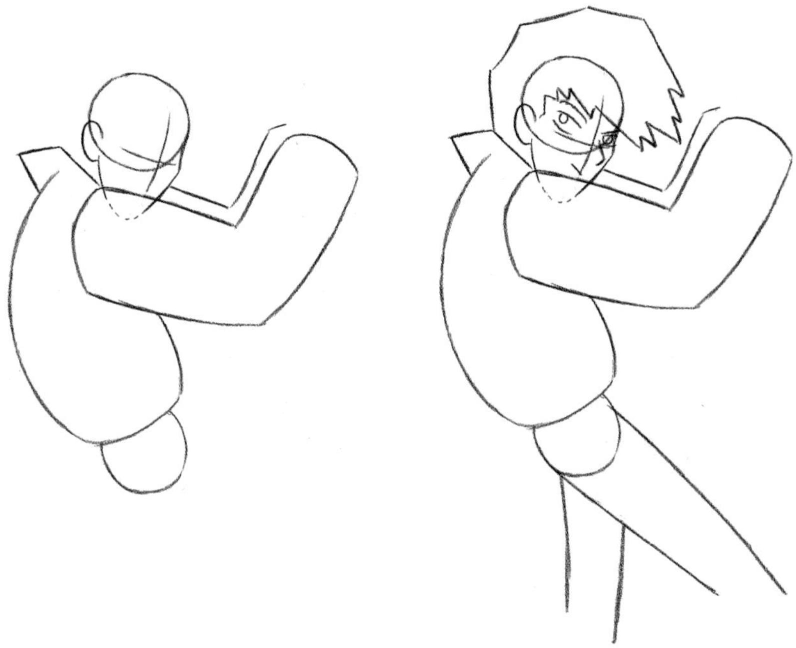

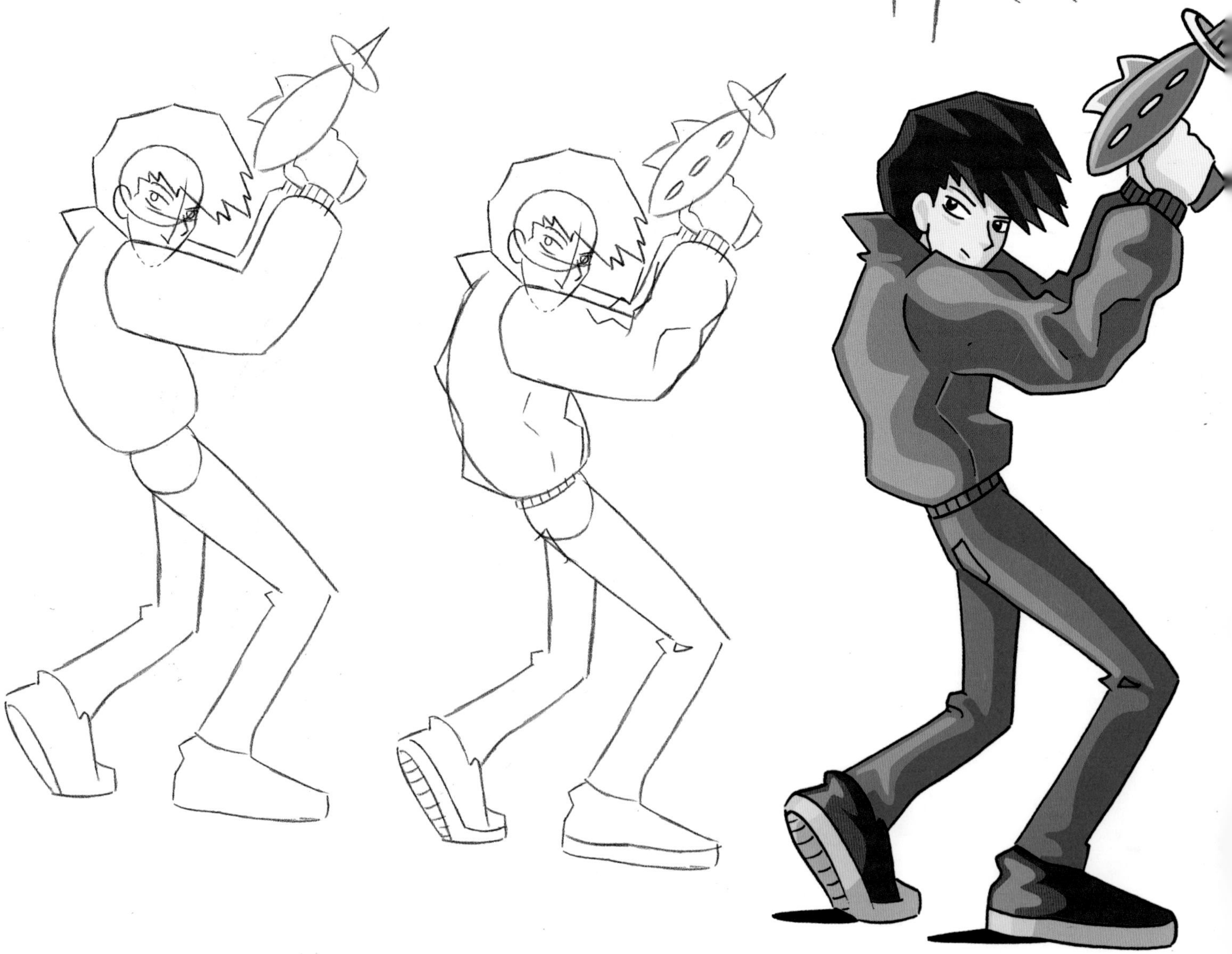

Manga Business Executive

She's a power broker in the corporate world. She wears a stylish suit, but nothing too flashy. High heels, jazzy earrings, and buttons on the sleeve complete her style.

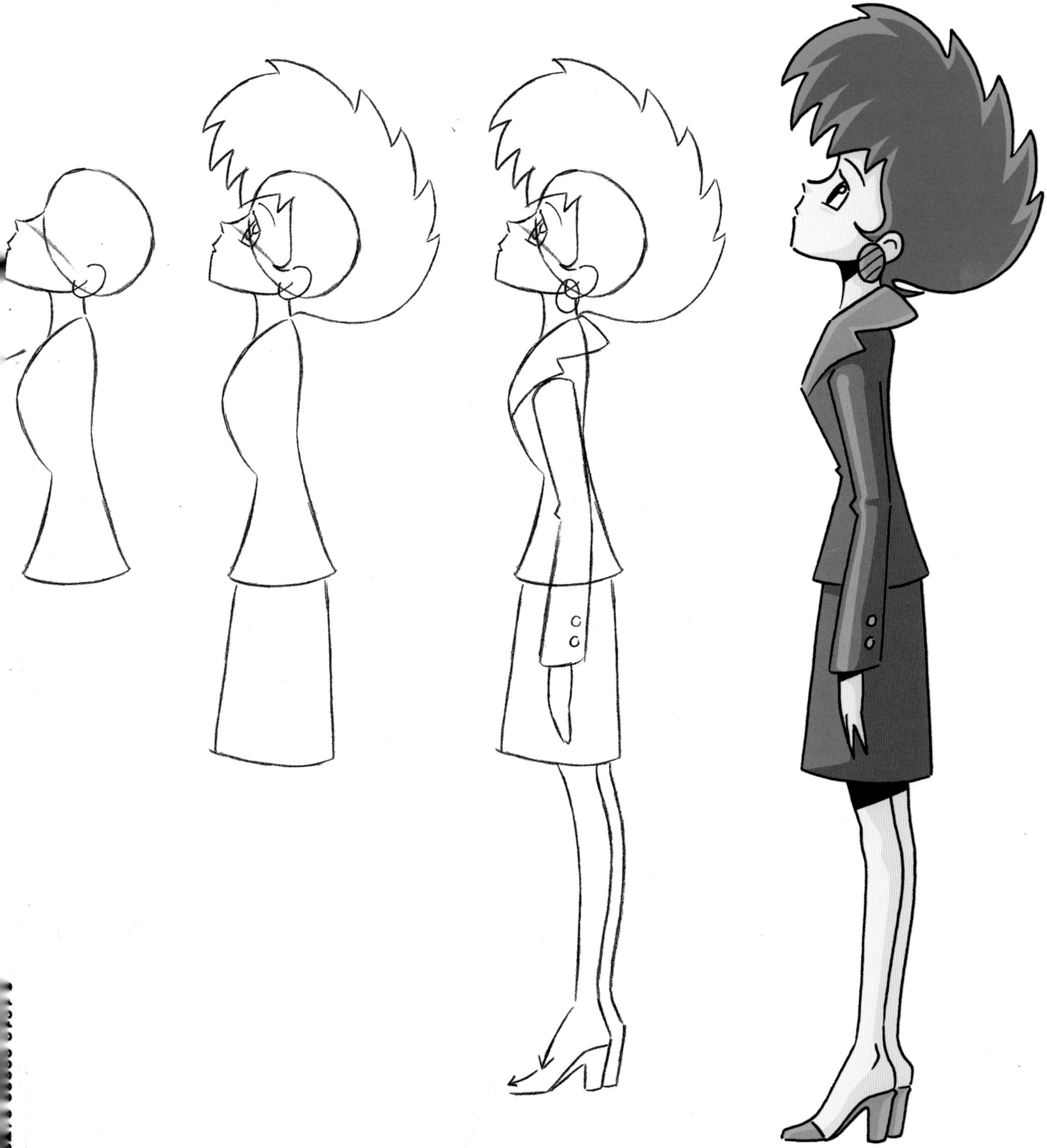

Mysterious Swordsman

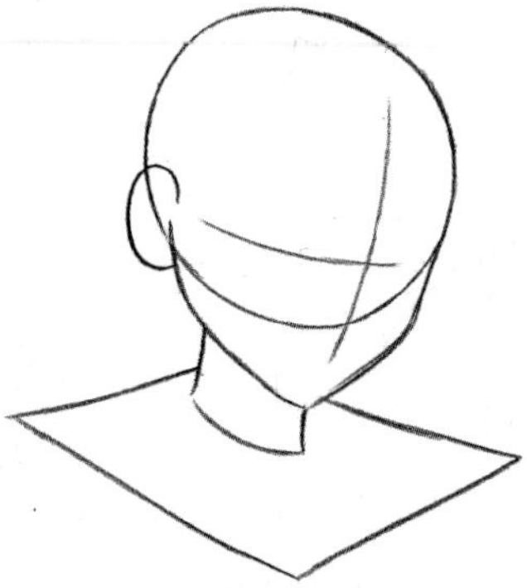

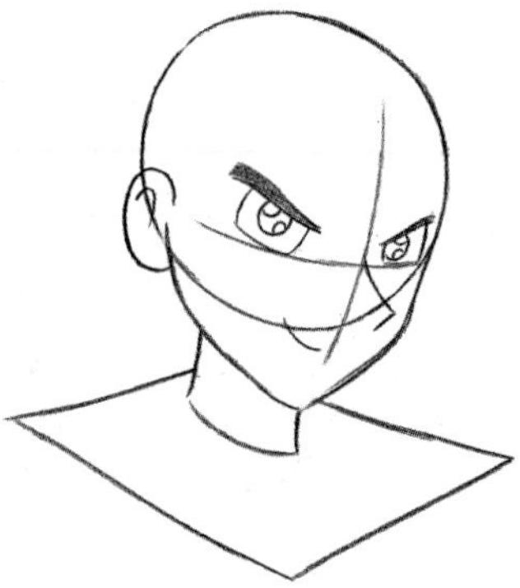

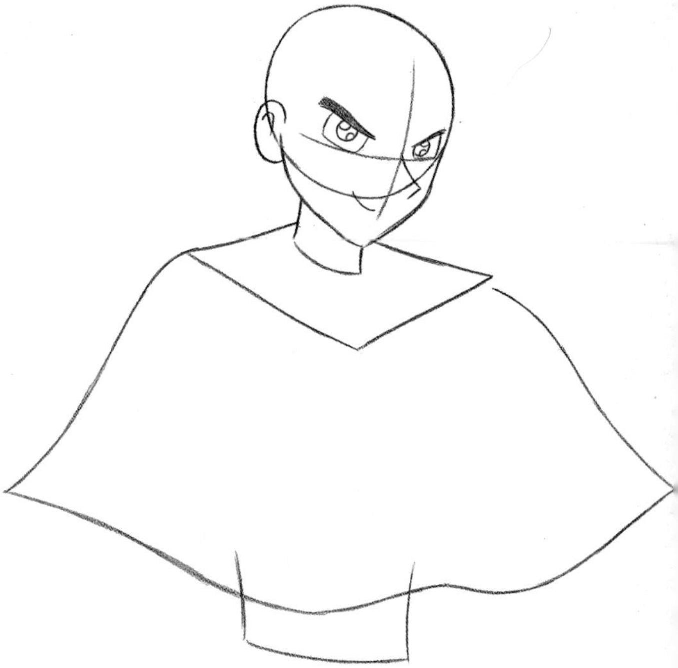

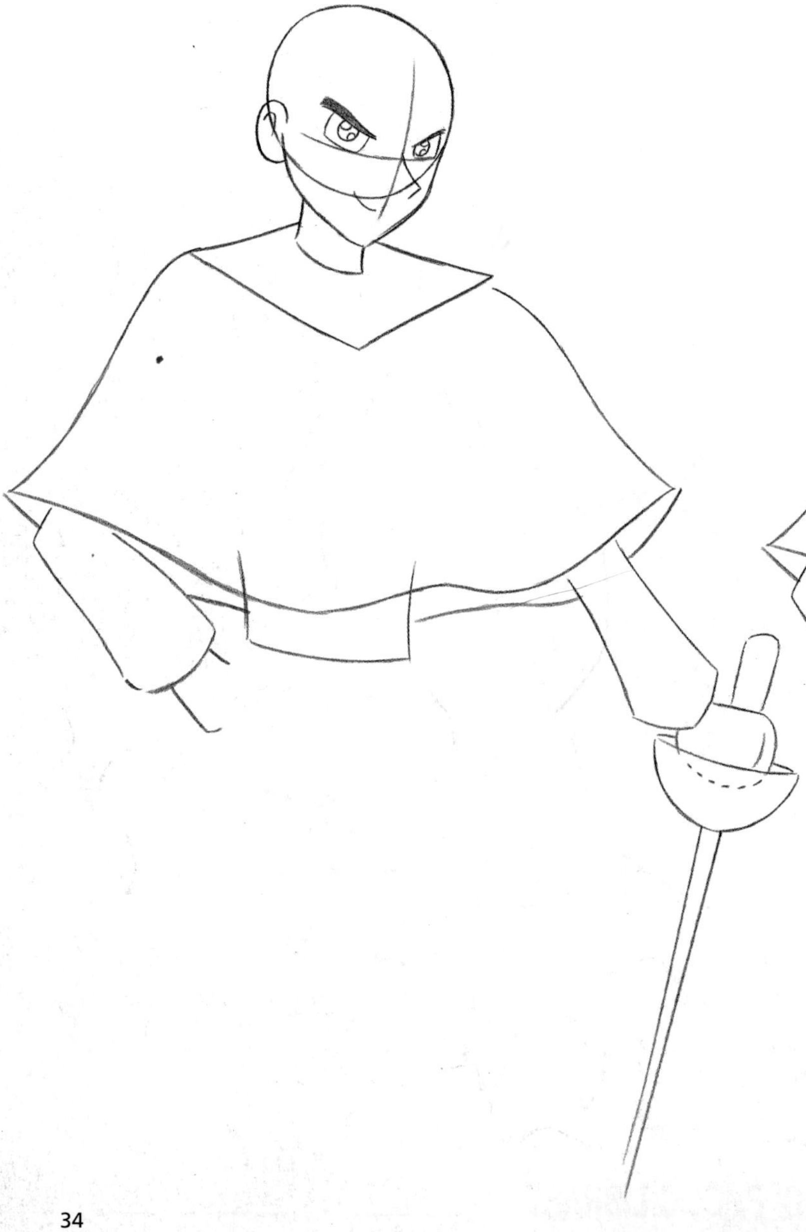

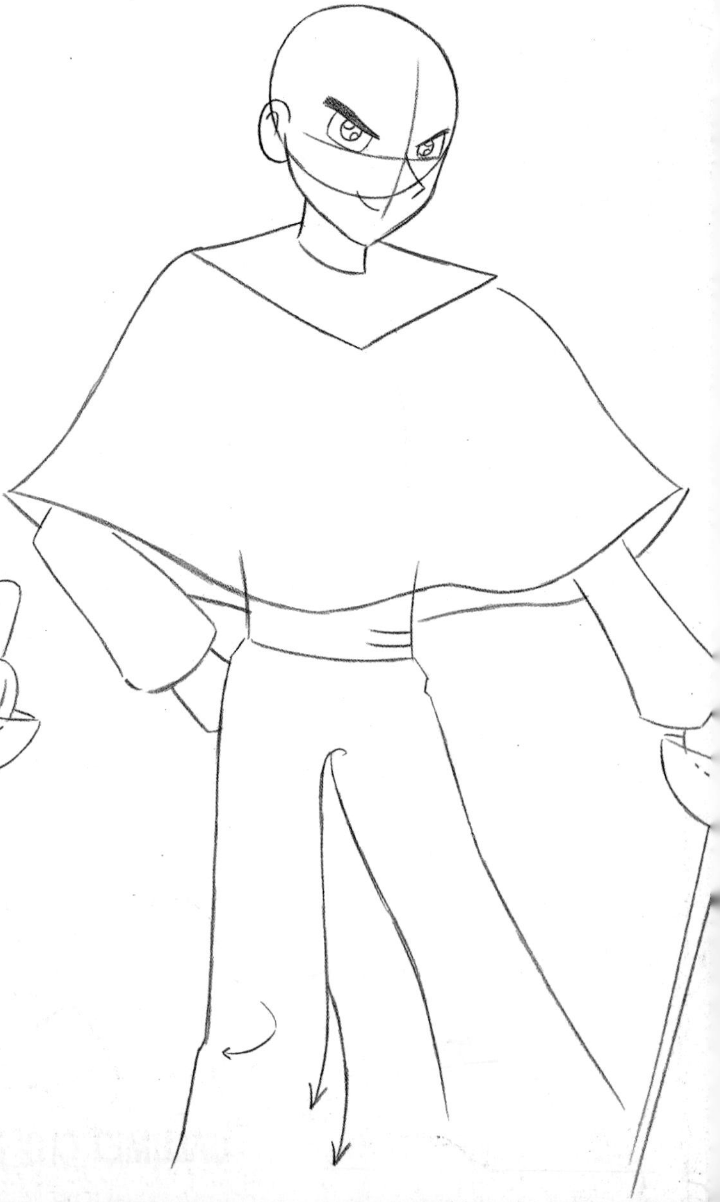

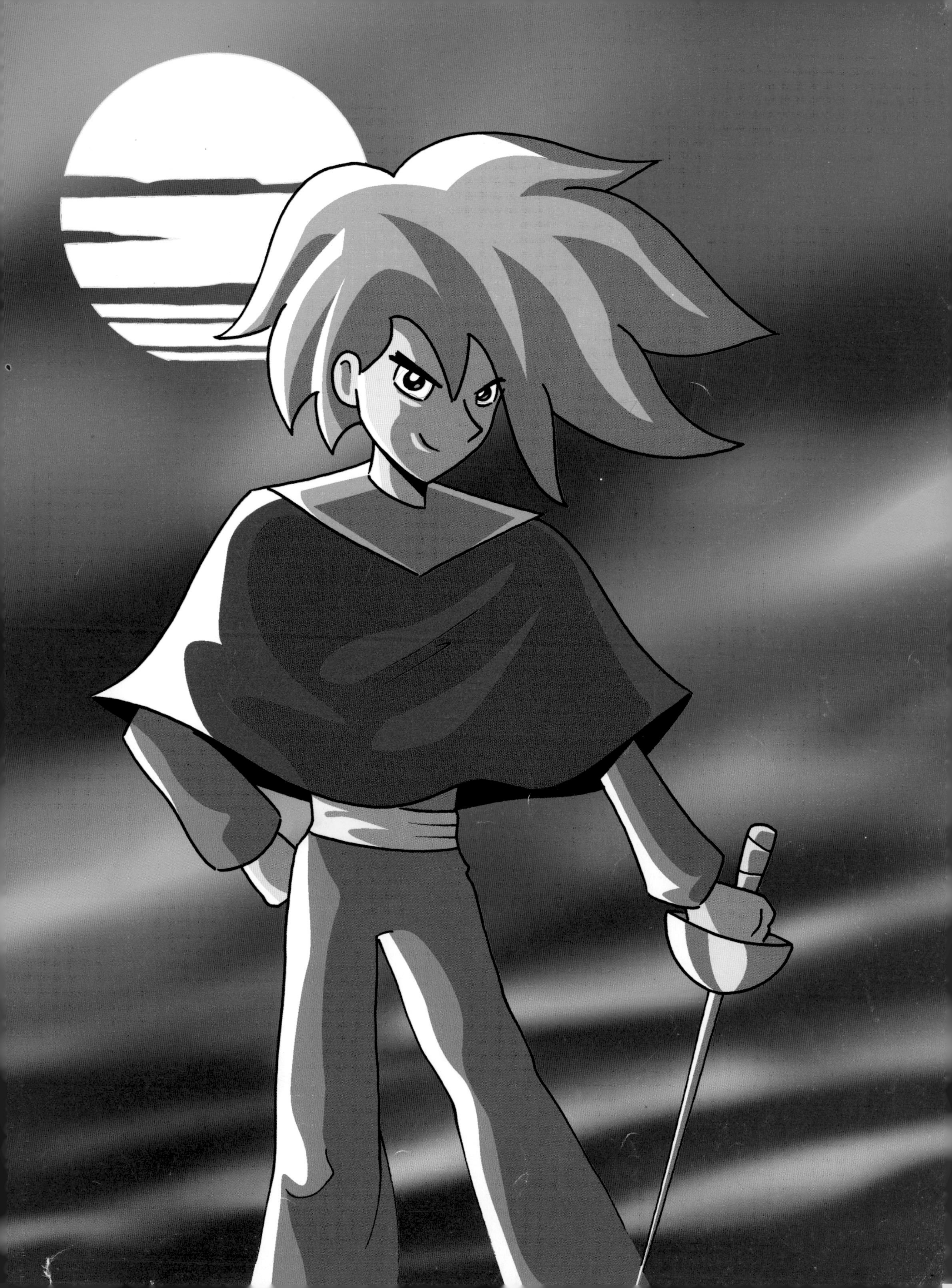

Homework Trouble

This poor girl can't figure out her class assignment, and her kitty can't figure out what's bothering her. I've broken the drawing down into lots of steps to help you.

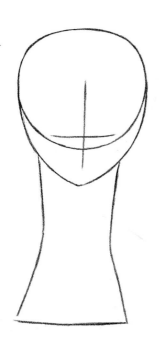

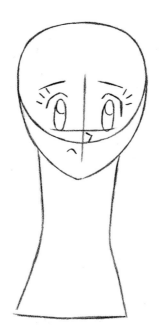

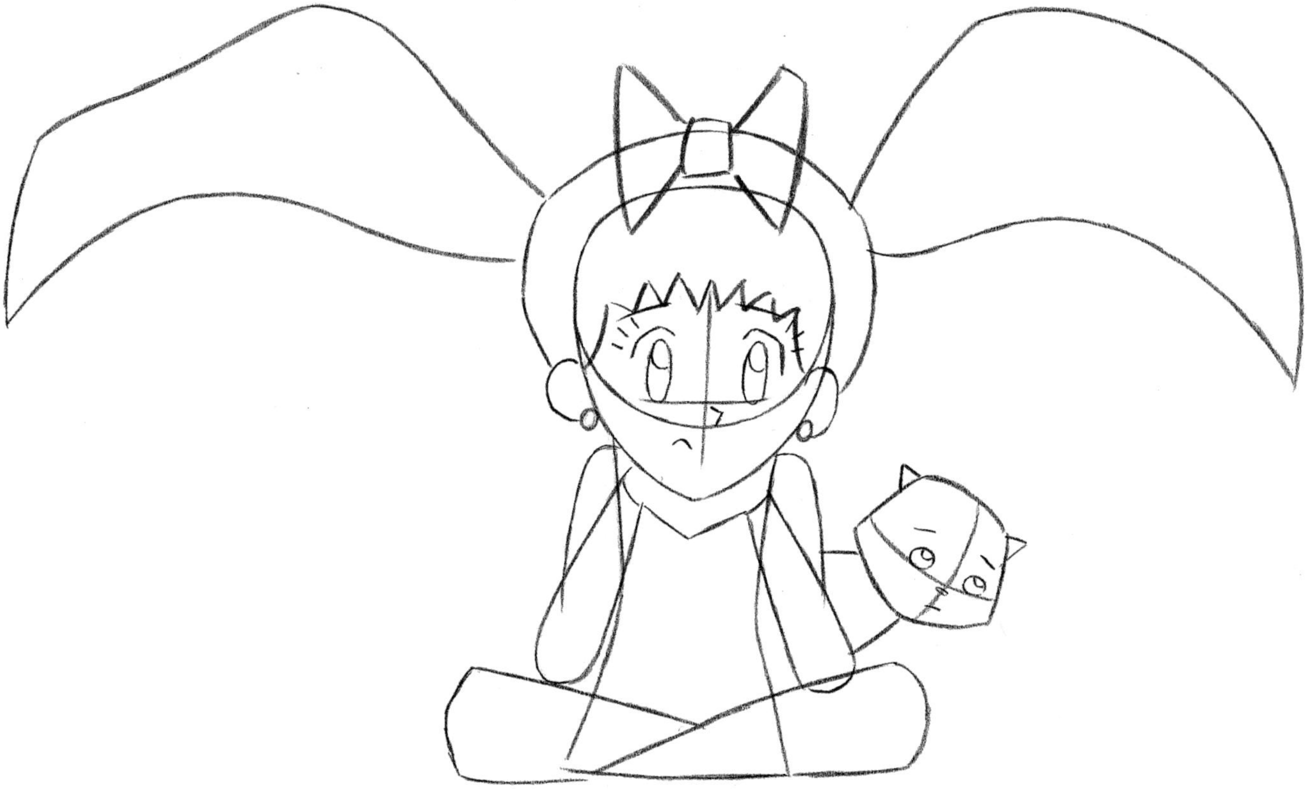

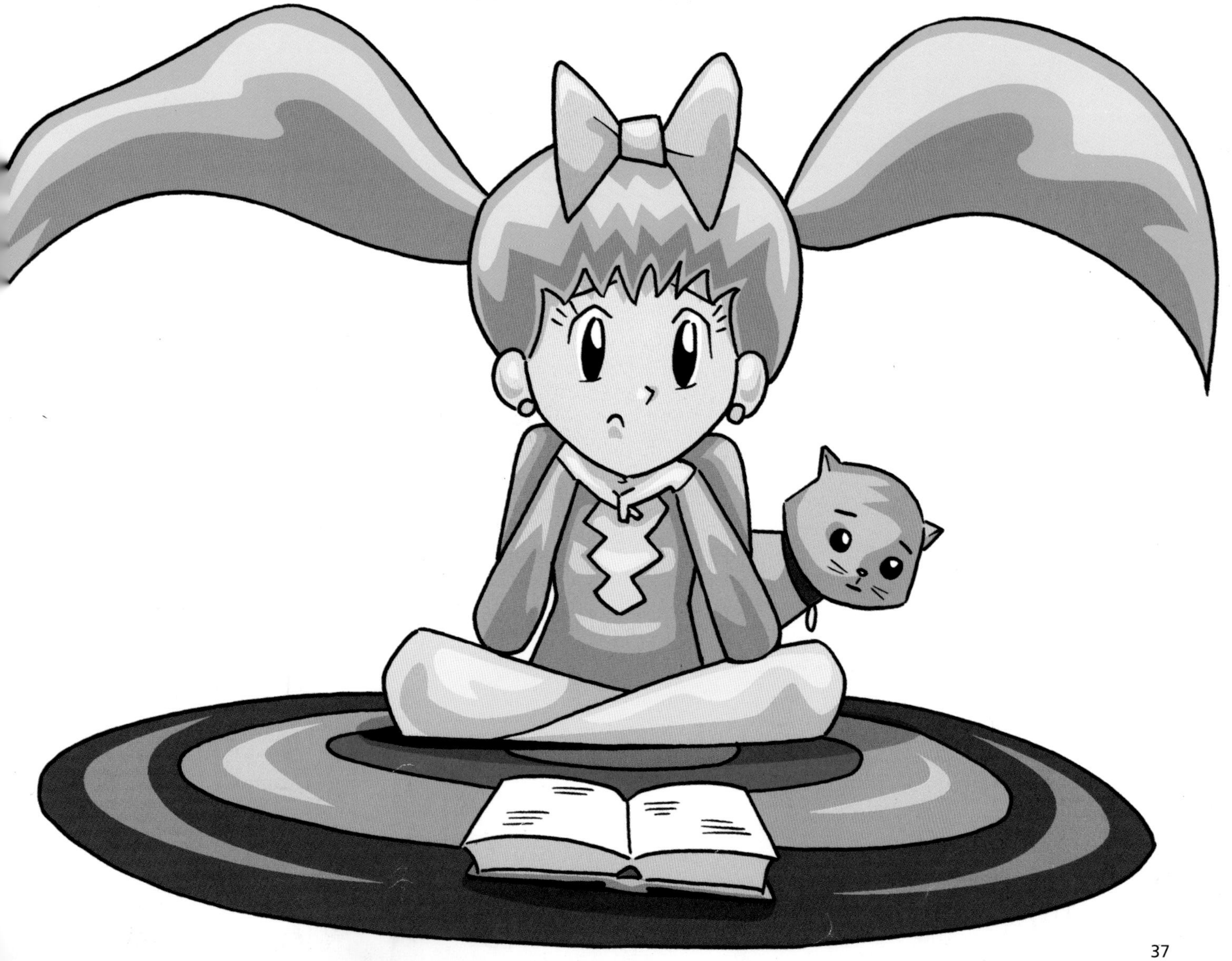

Hero Knight

I've given this knight windblown hair to make him look more dramatic. Make sure all of the hair blows in the same direction or it will look strange. His heavy sword tells us that he must be strong, as do his extra-wide shoulders.

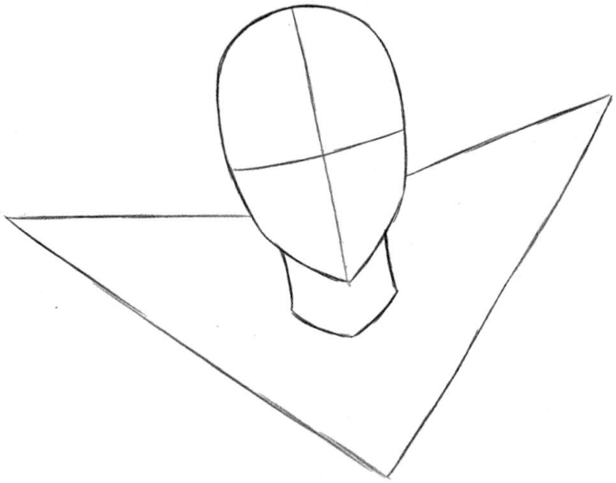

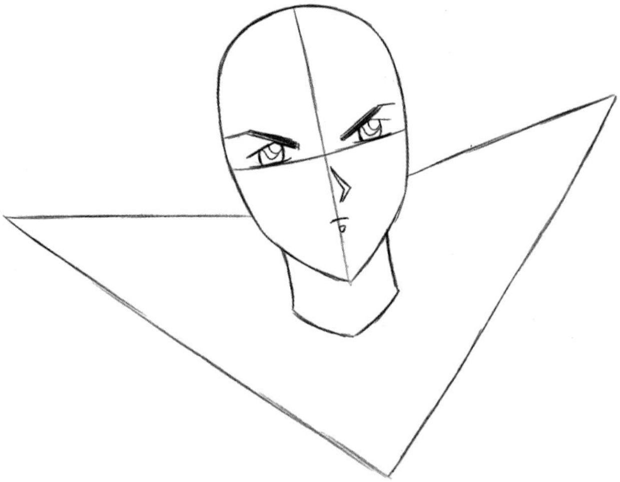

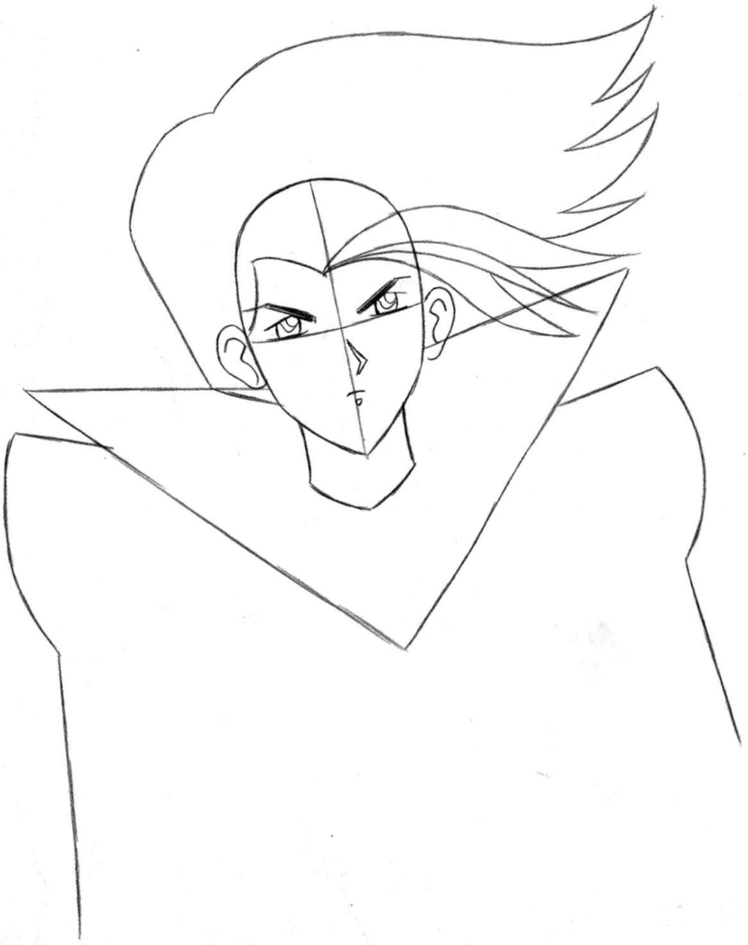

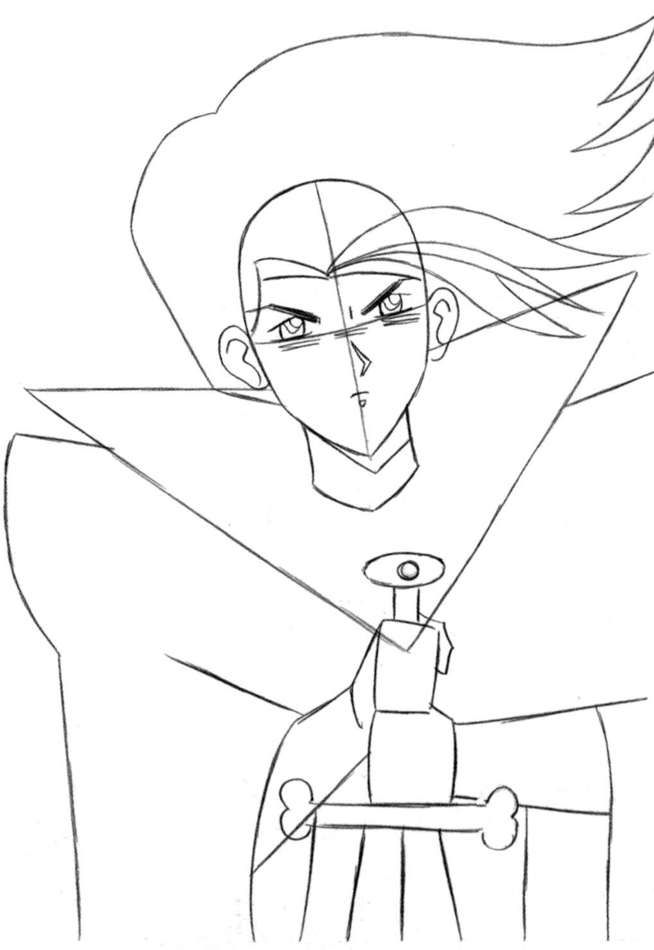

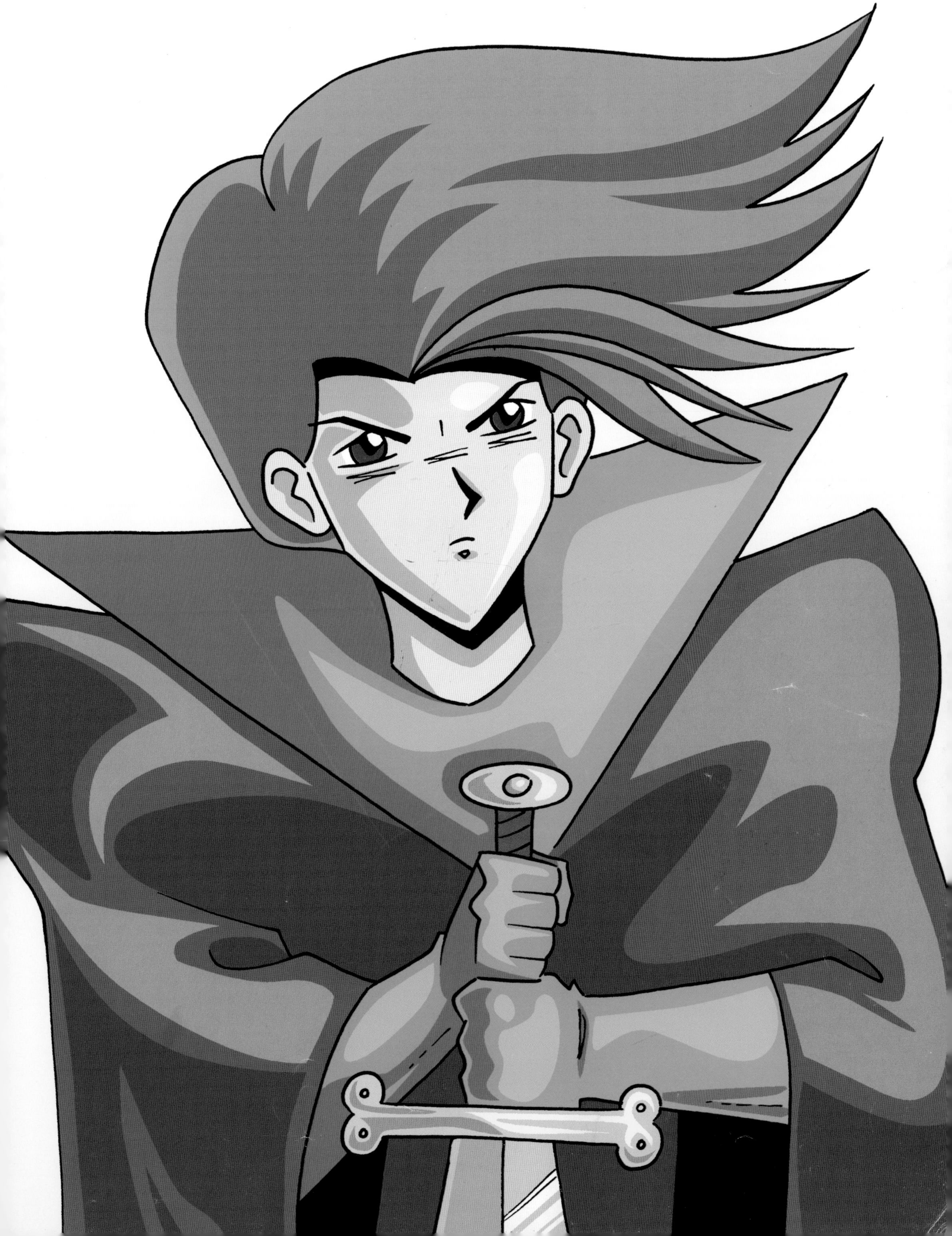

Laser Blast

Try to be creative with your special effects! You can draw lasers as streams, waves, or even pellets.

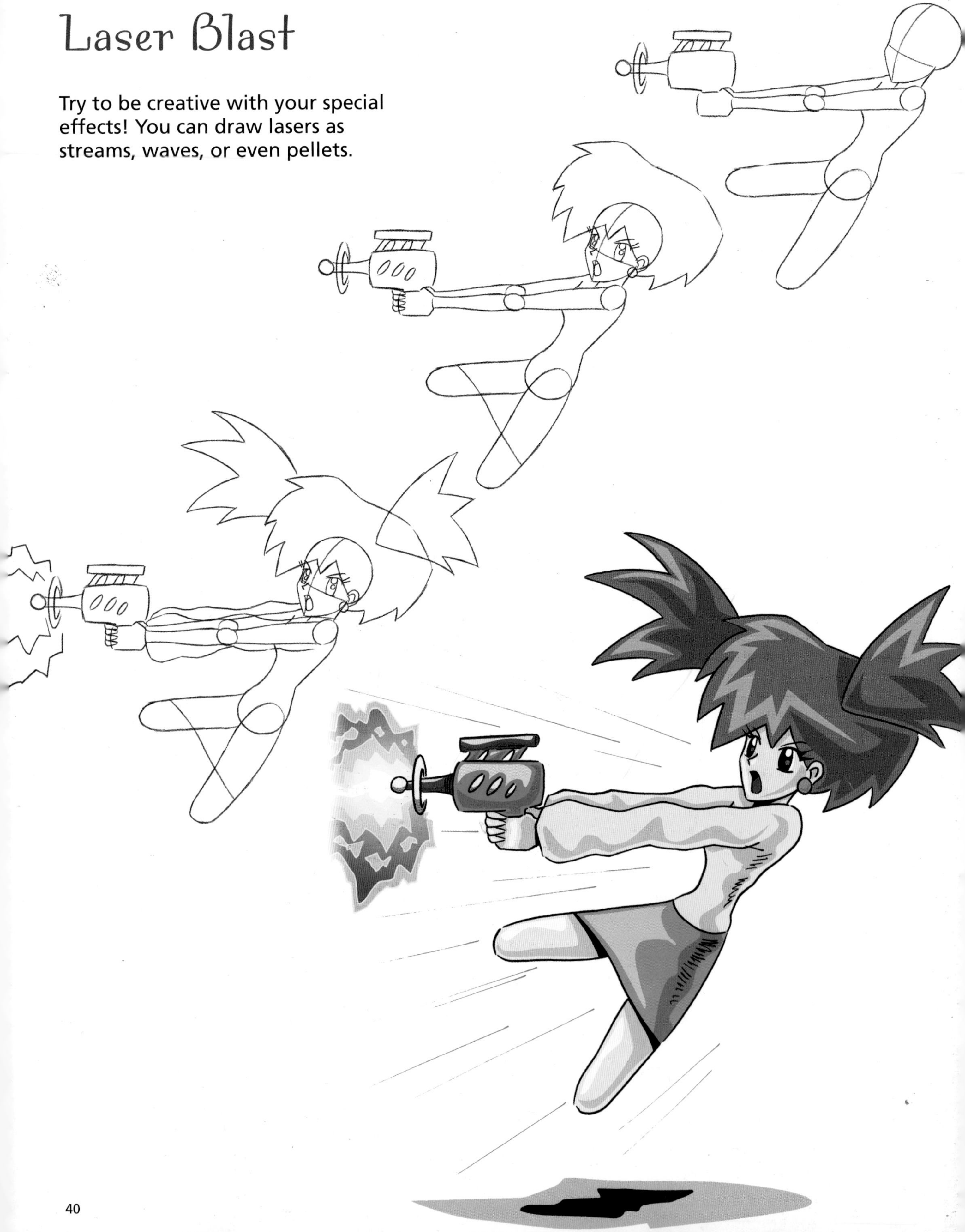

Leader of the Earth Rebels

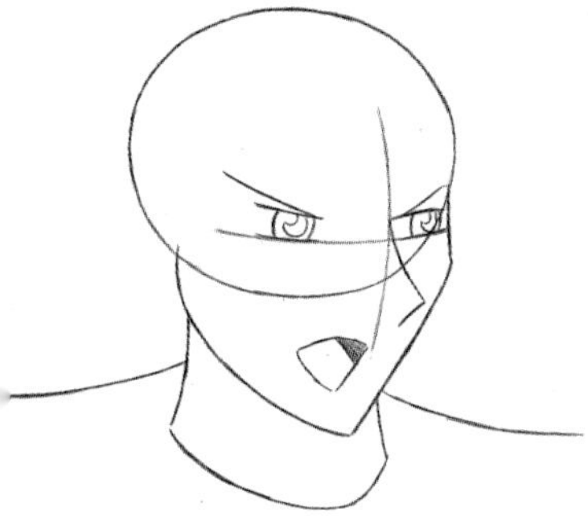

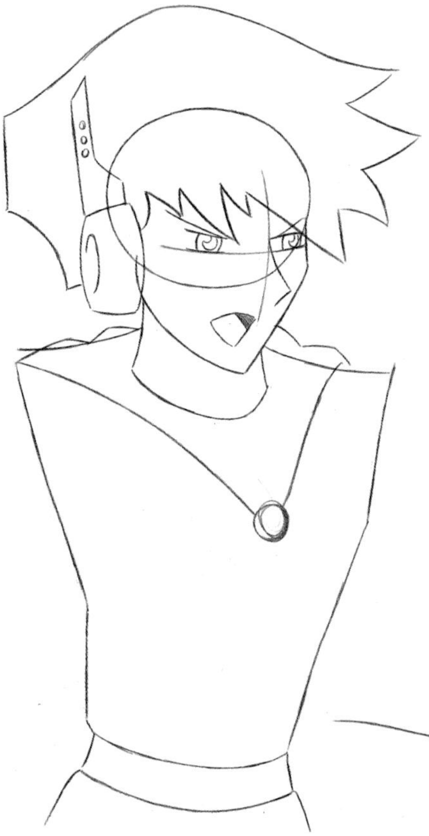

A rebel leader has just gotta have a headset. That way he can bark orders while striking cool poses, like this one. I like to put a little scratch-mark, like a scar, on the faces of rebels and their leaders, to make them look scrappy.

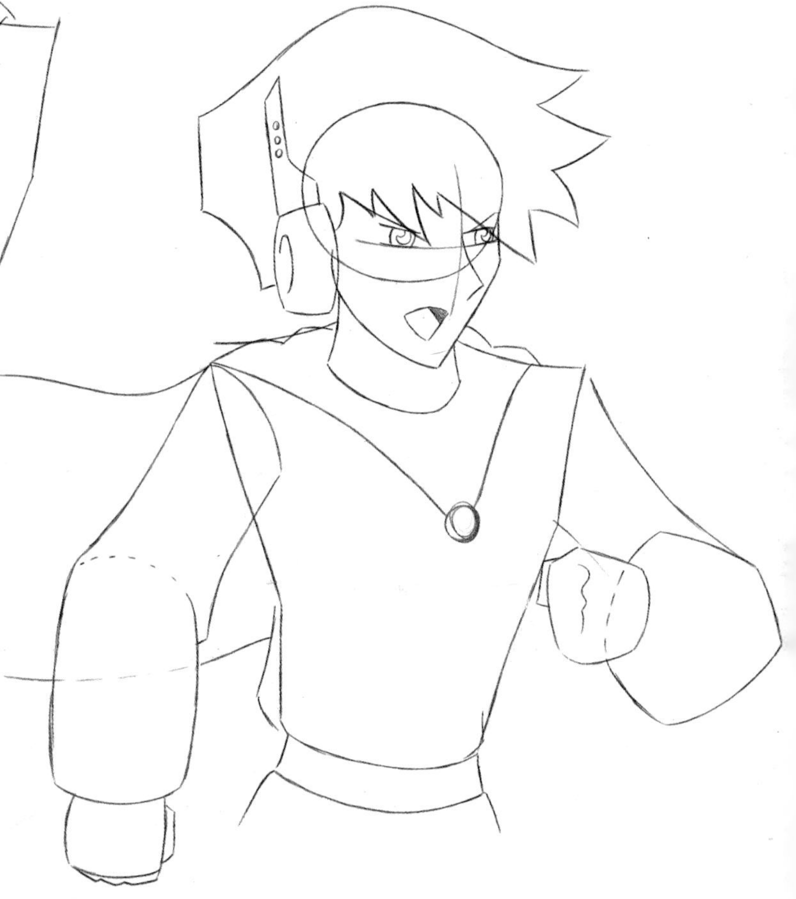

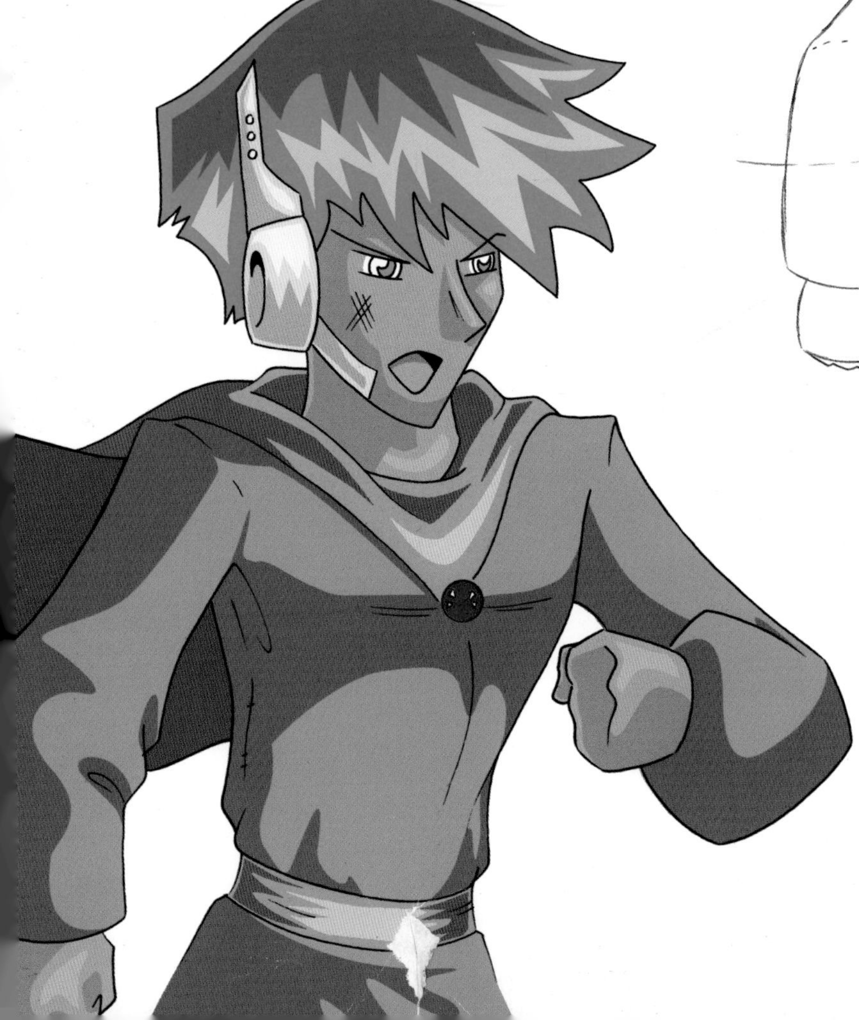

Magic Sorceress

Evil characters always get to wear the flashy clothes. Look at how fancy her outfit is. Villains are *never* modest!

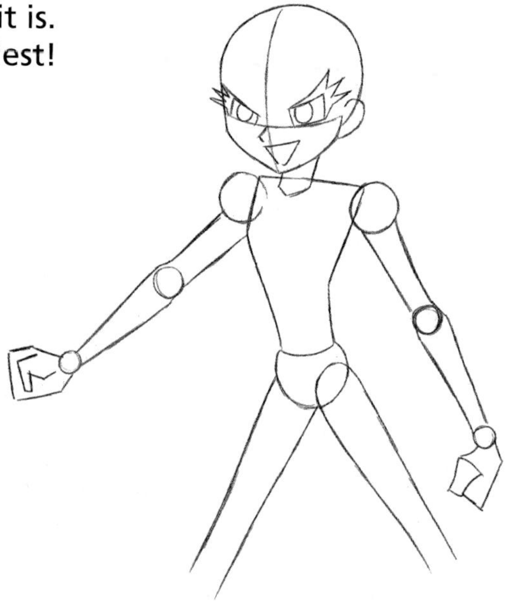

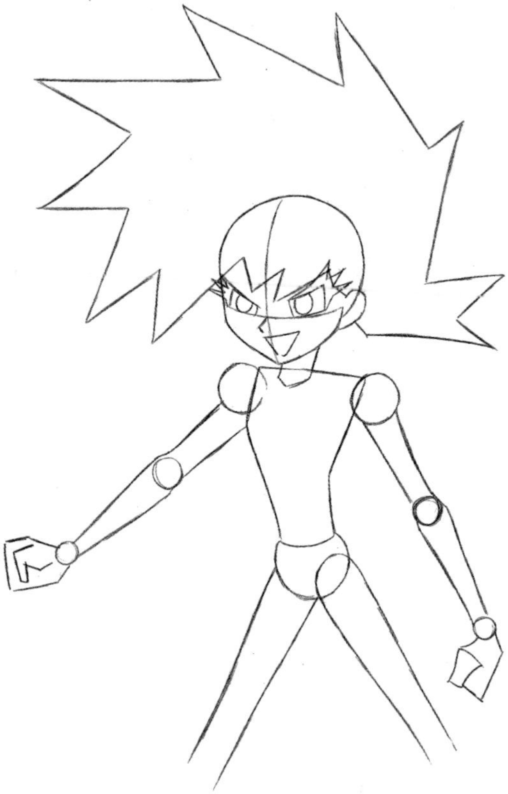

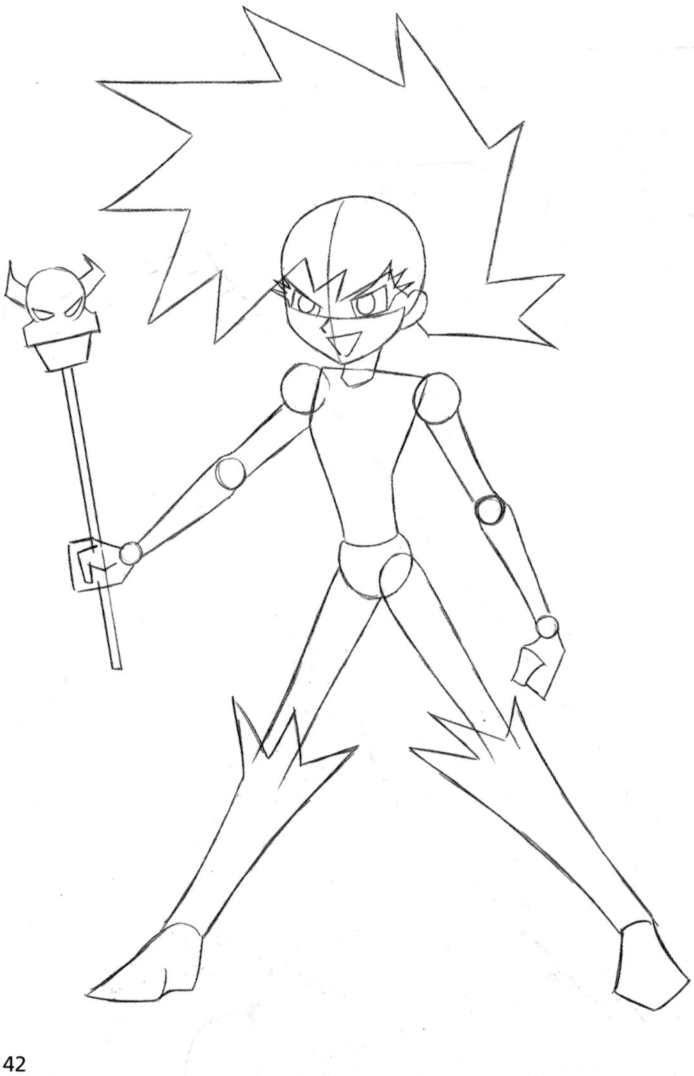

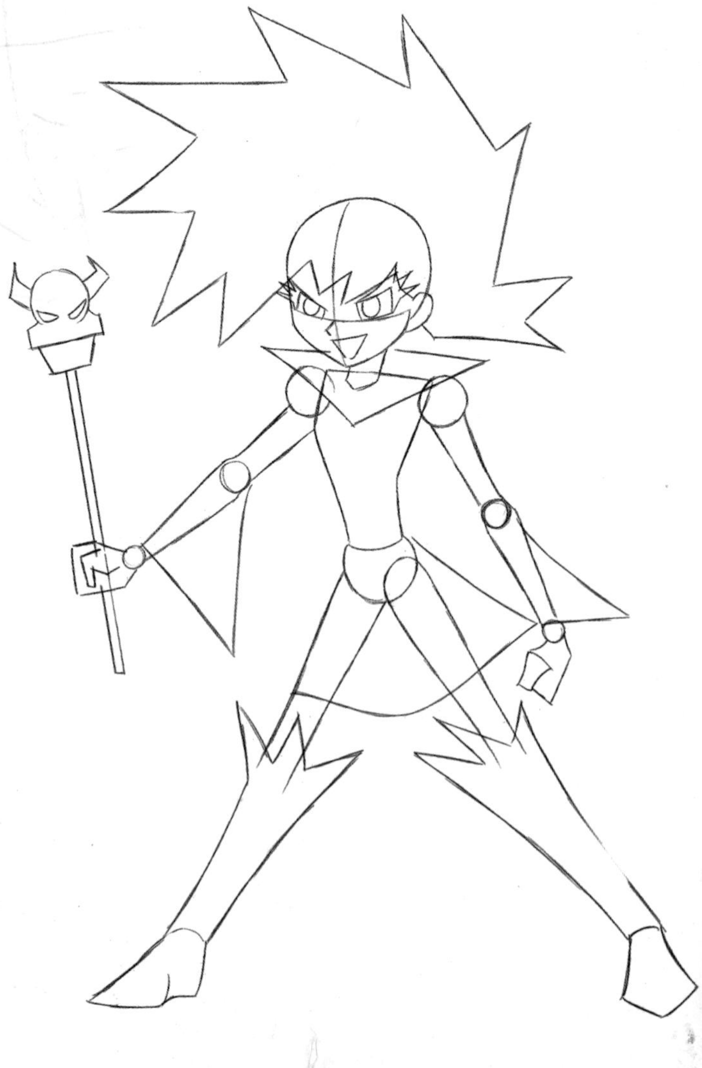

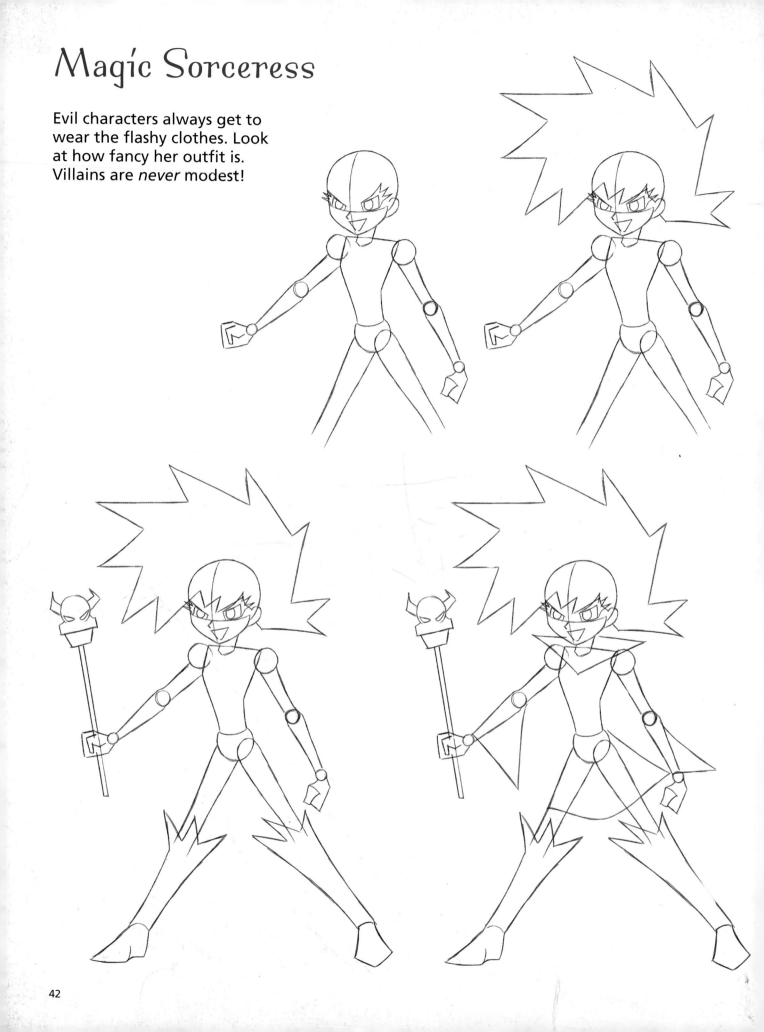

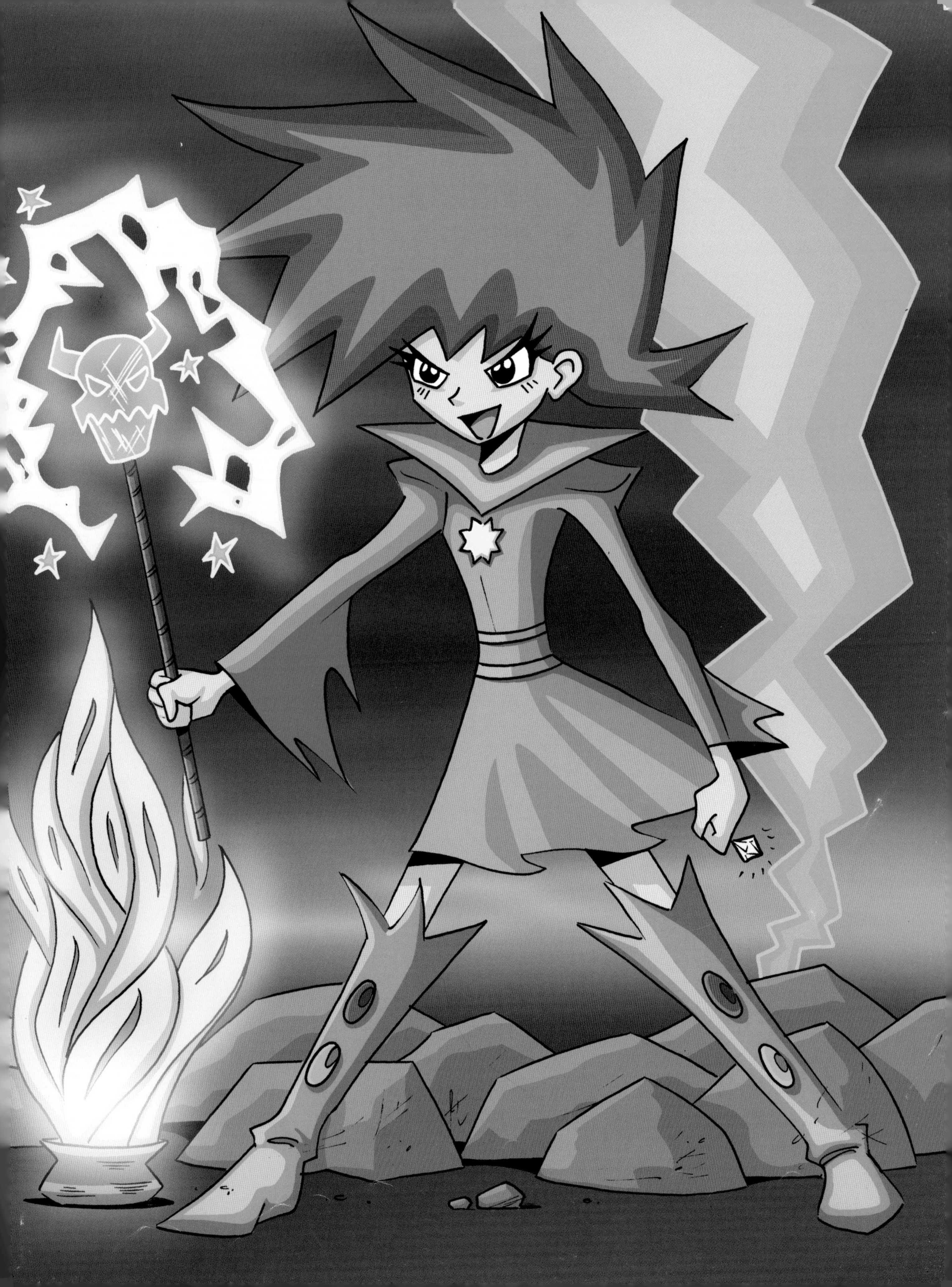

THE BATTLING ROBOTS OF MANGA

Awesome giant robots are among the most popular and exciting characters in manga. You might think they look hard to draw, but they're not! If you can draw circles, ovals, rectangles, and squares, you can draw giant robots.

Mr. Colossus

Start with basic shapes and save the details for last. It's only in the last step that we get kind of fancy. Everything else is a matter of plopping one big shape on top of another.

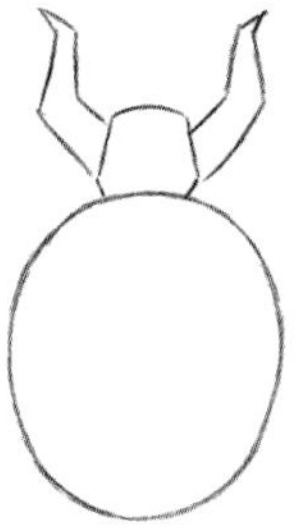

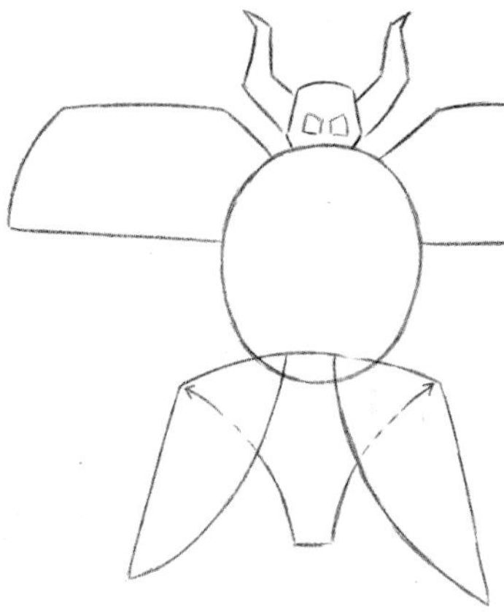

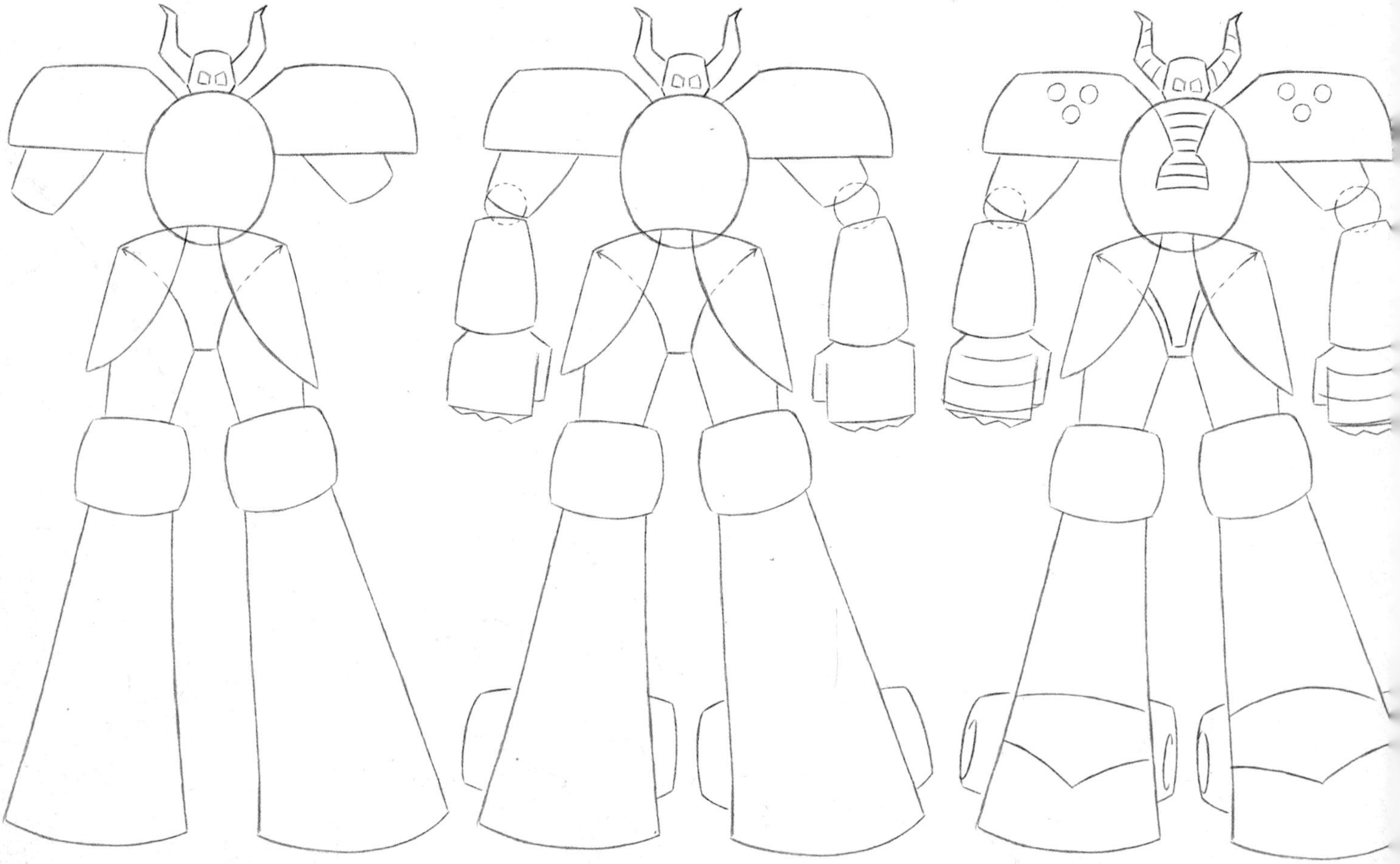

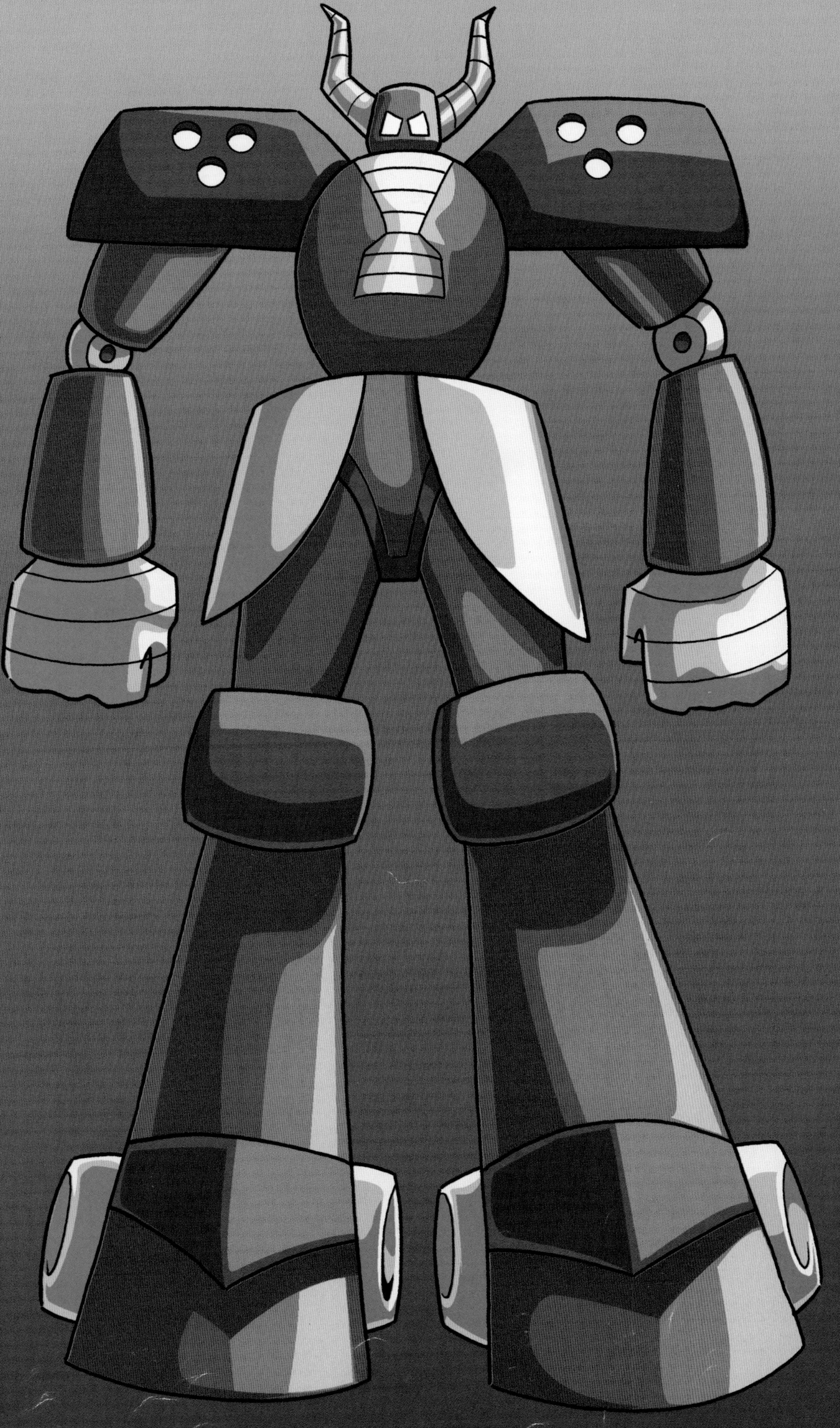

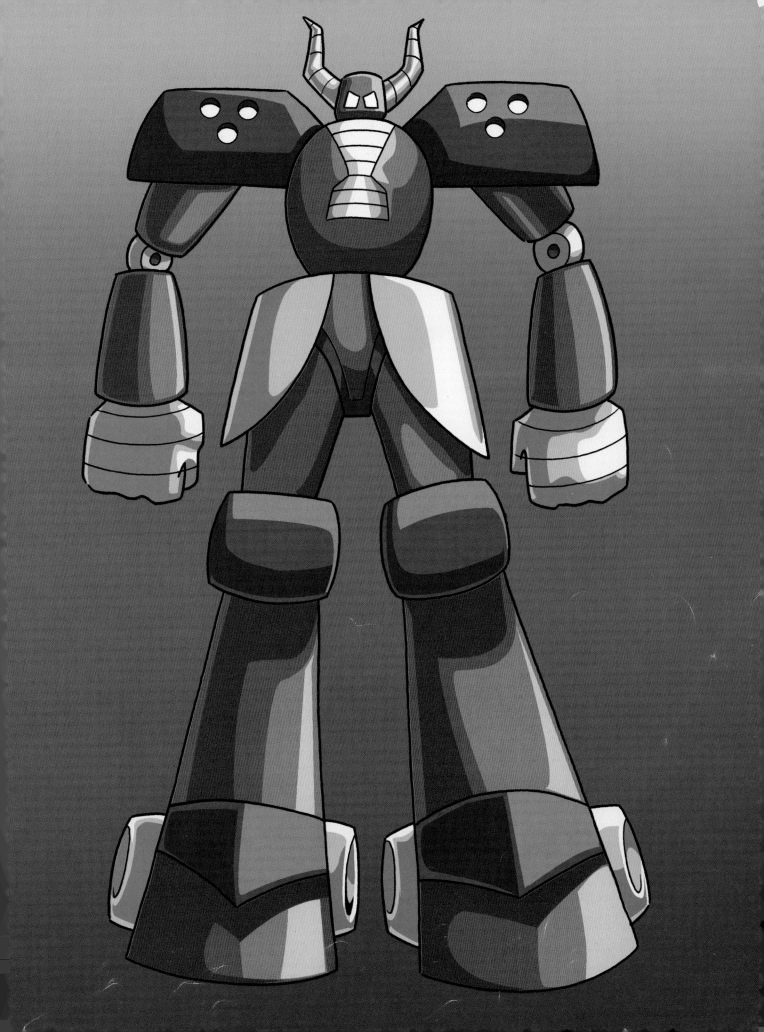

Using Arms as Weapons

Giant robots don't need to carry weapons—they *are* weapons! This powerful robot has forearms that are, in fact, laser rifles. Now, look at his eyes. Okay, so maybe he doesn't have eyes, but he has an eye guard. See how it makes a "V"? A "V" is the natural shape of a frown, and is often used for robot eyes. It makes the robot look intense. You want that in a giant robot.

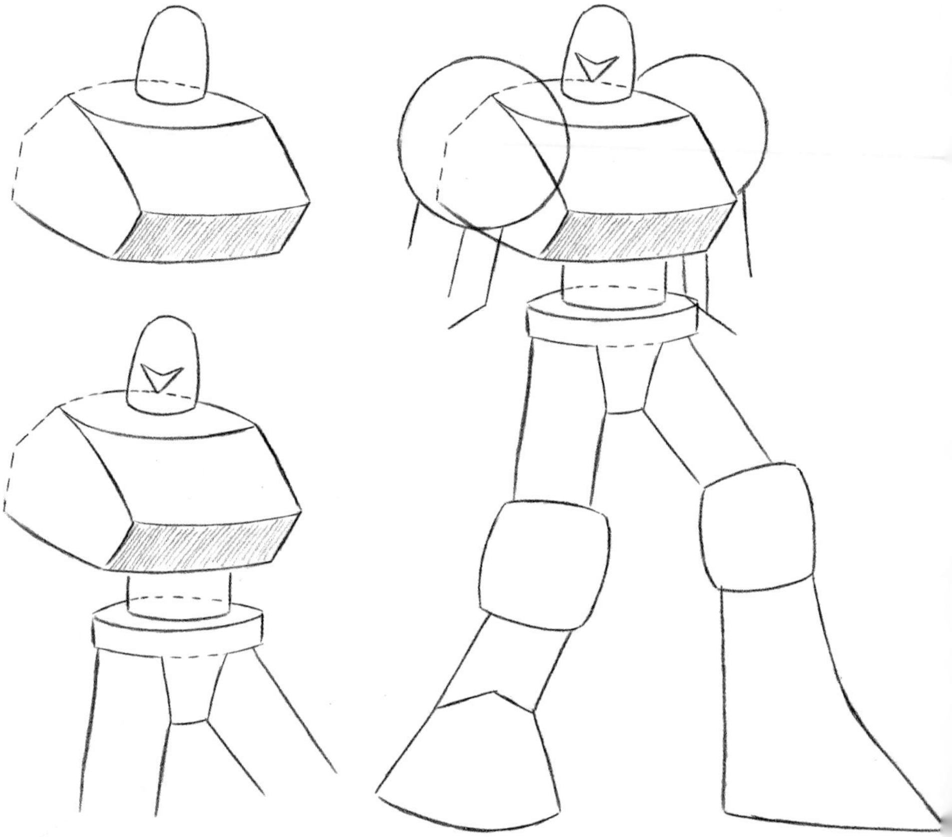

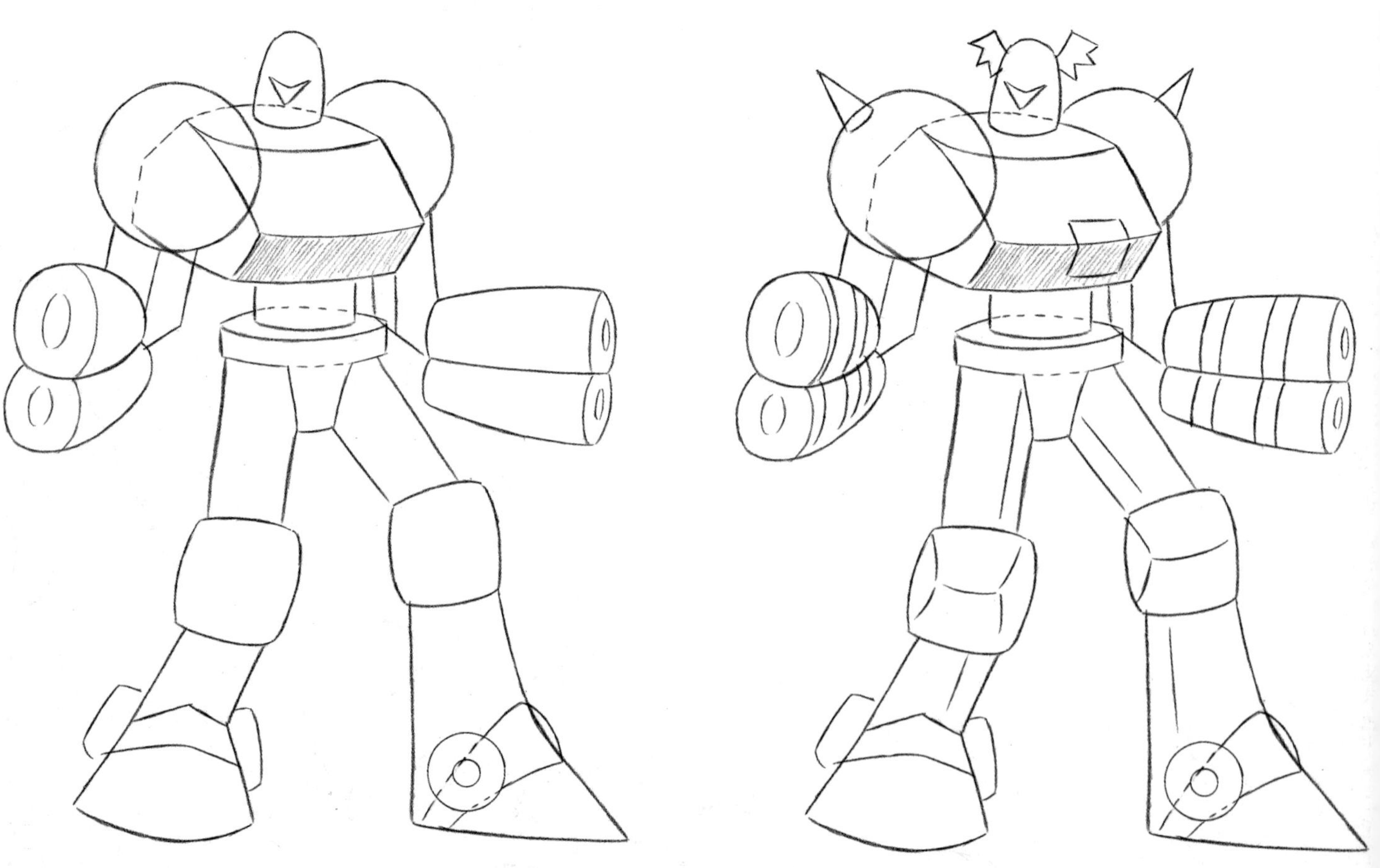

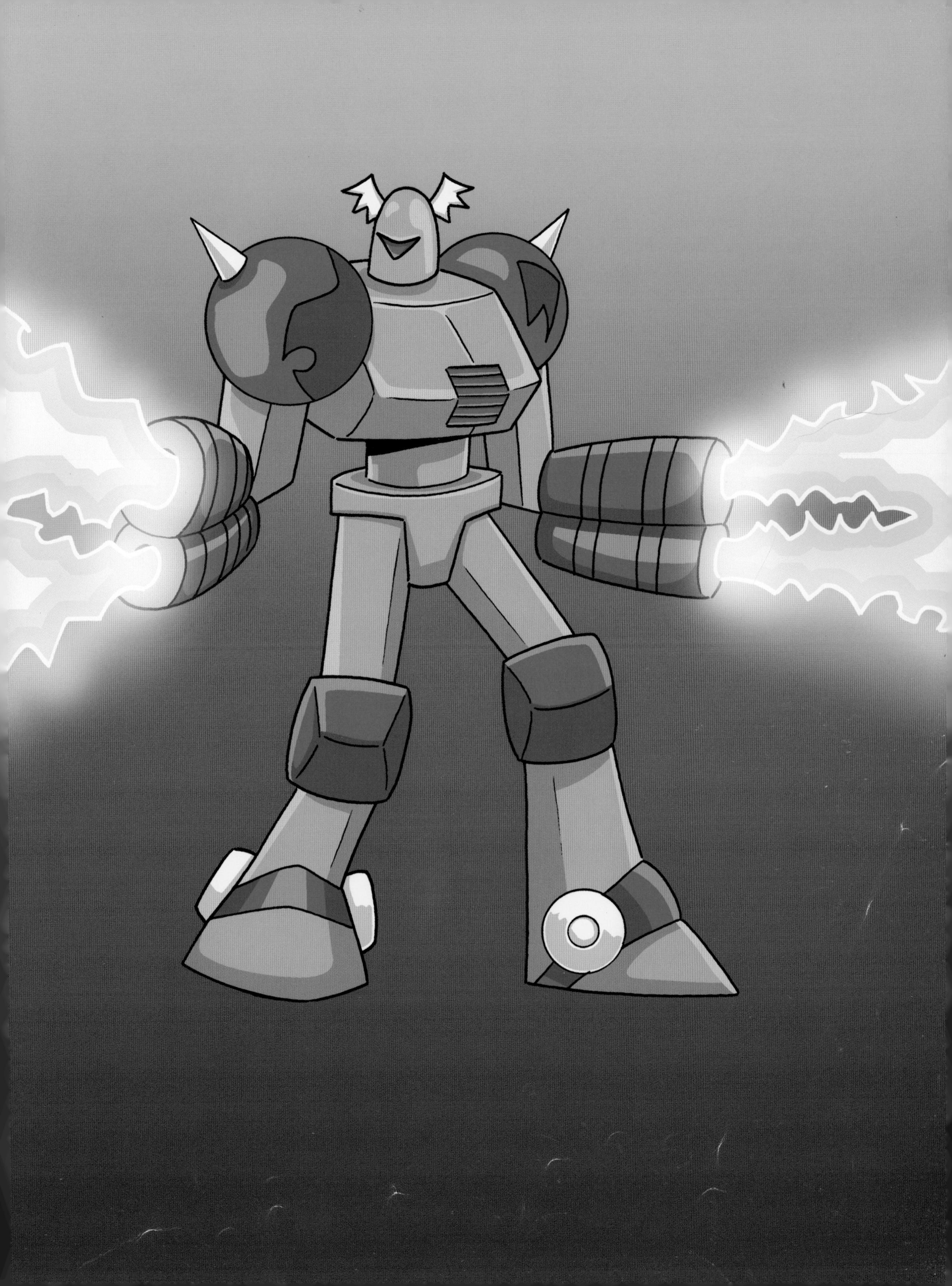

Flying Robot Soldier

The main part of this robot's body is an *octagon,* which is a shape with eight sides. Don't worry if each little section doesn't look exactly right—it's the overall effect we're after. Oh, and when you draw wings on a giant robot—any giant robot—make them huge. Little wings aren't impressive enough.

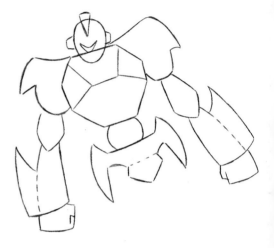

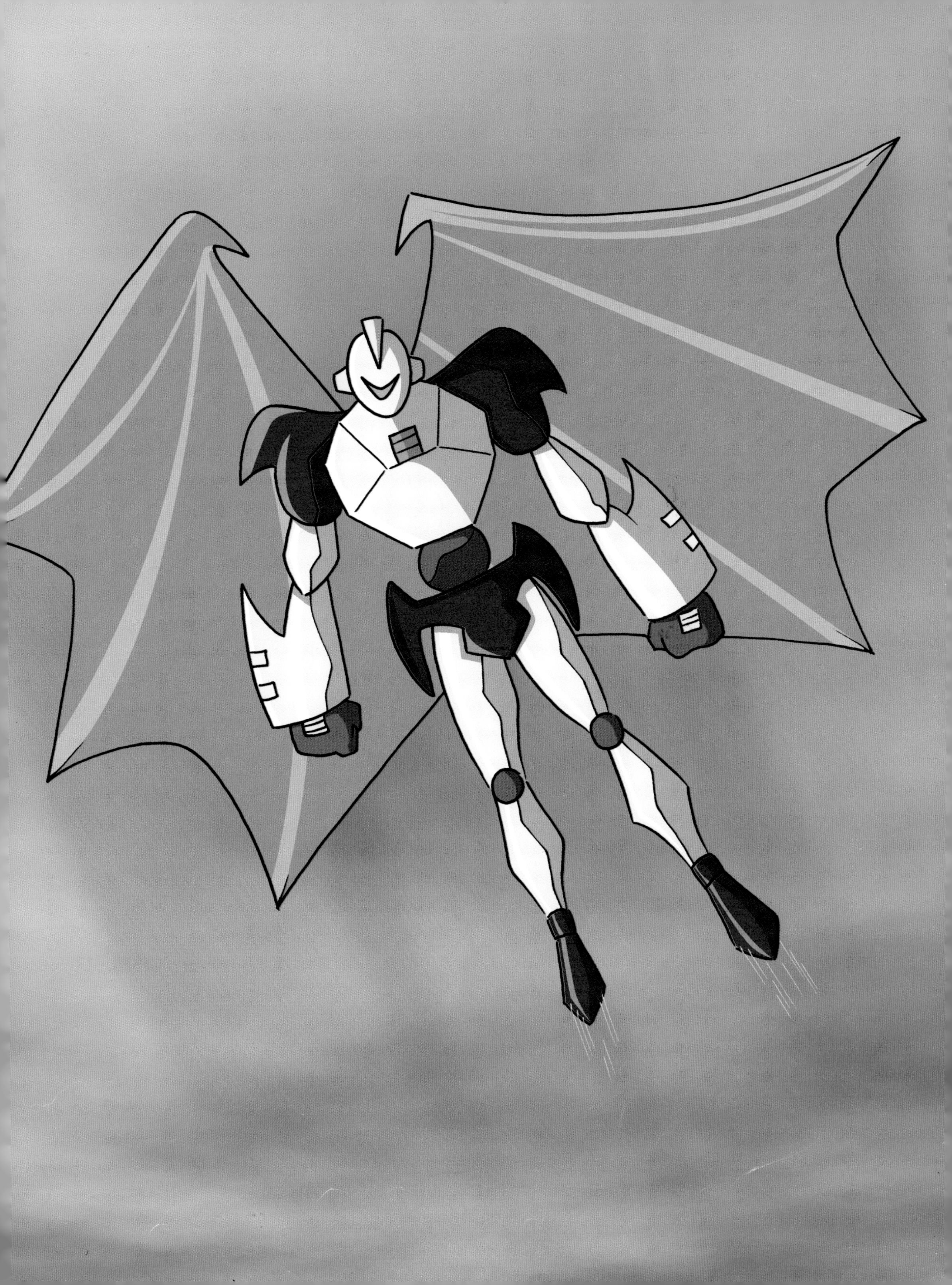

Laser Fighter

Doesn't this robot look intense? Want to know why? Simple: I gave him a big chest and made him really tall, but then gave him a tiny, mechanical-looking head. That makes him look like a fighting machine that is all strength without much smarts. Like a system programmed to destroy.

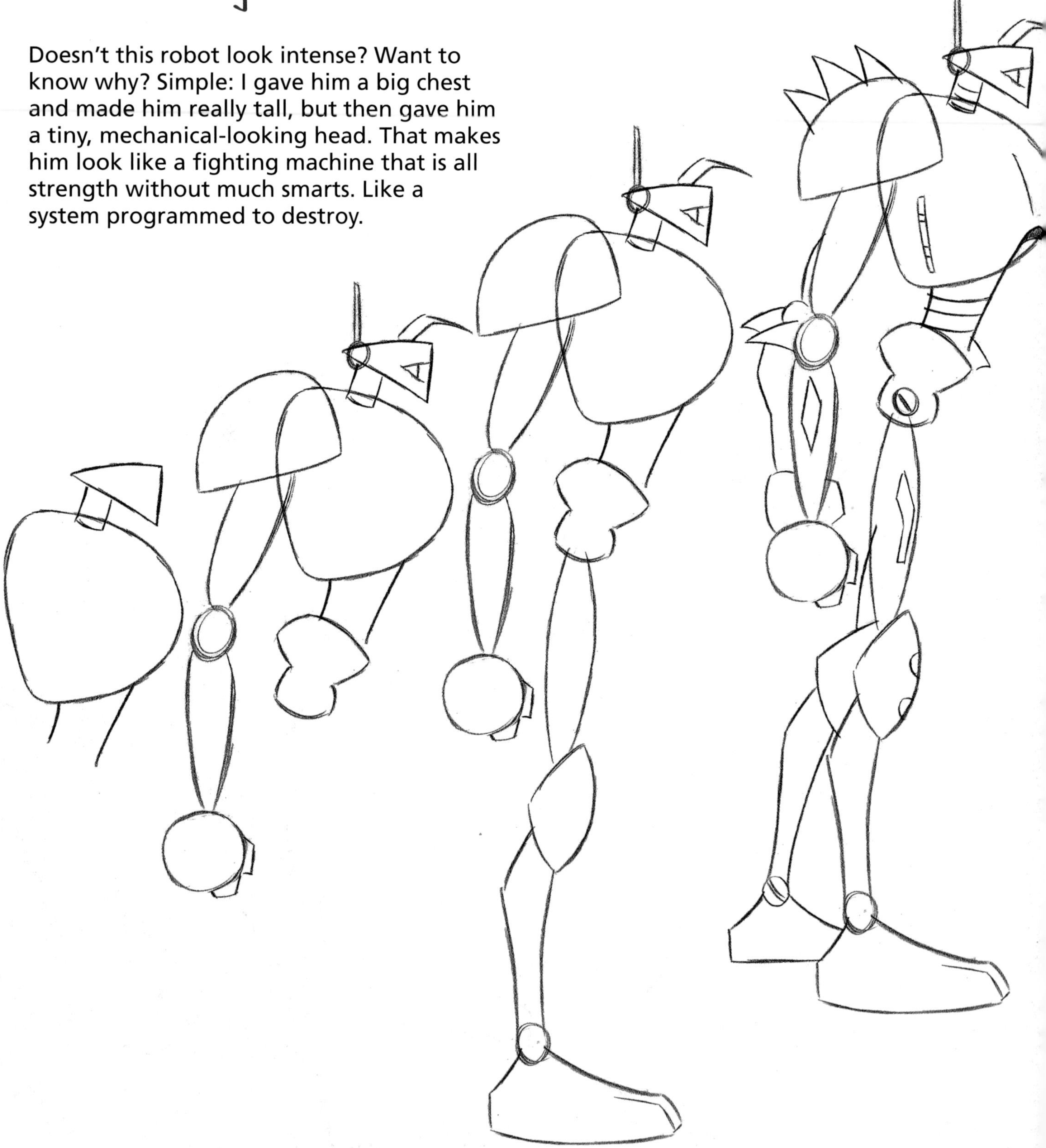

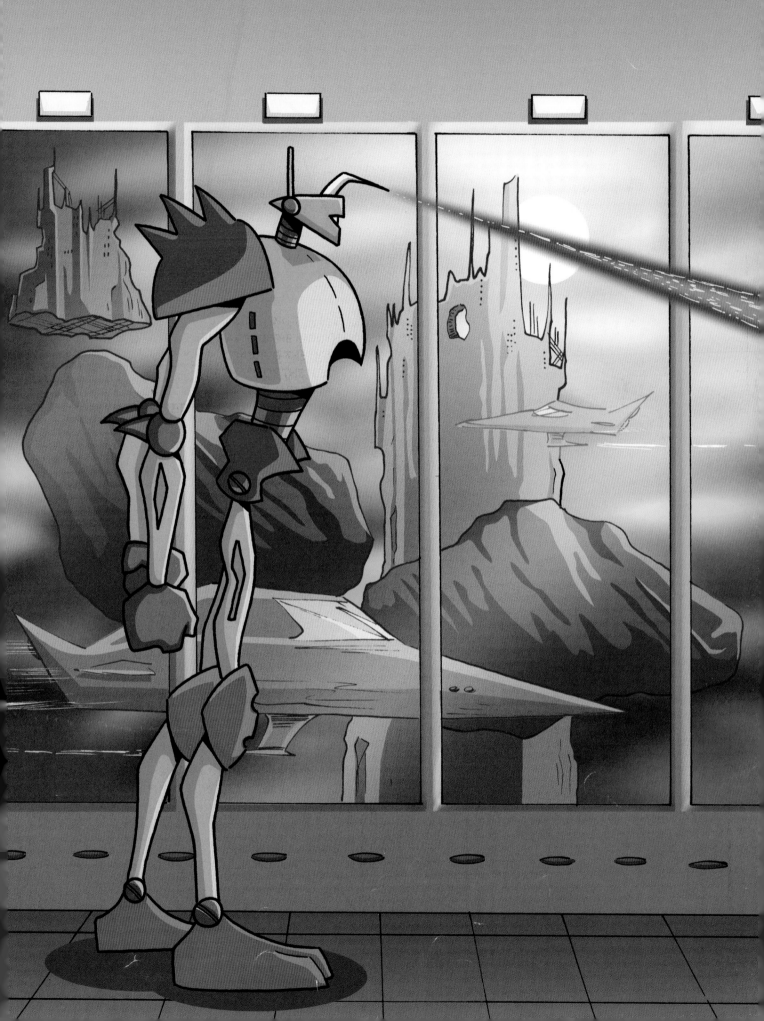

BONUS SECTION: ADVANCED DRAWINGS

Once you get the hang of drawing manga characters (and I know you will!), you may want to try something a little more challenging. These drawings may take a bit more practice, but they'll look great when you're done.

Extreme Perspective

In this drawing, everything looks like it's coming right at you. Here's the trick: Draw a big upper body, but tiny legs. And notice how the chest hides the stomach area completely—we don't even see it.

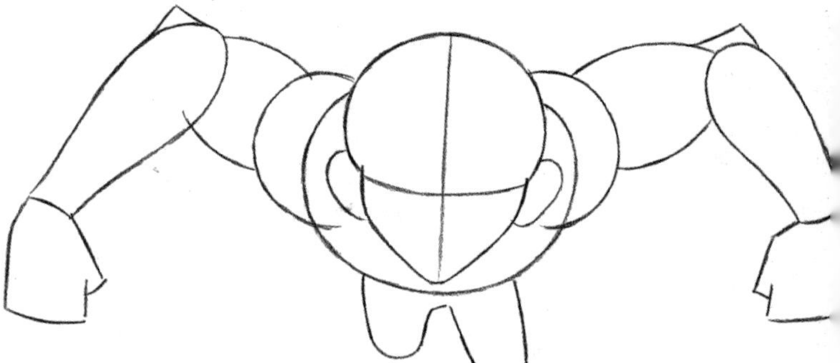

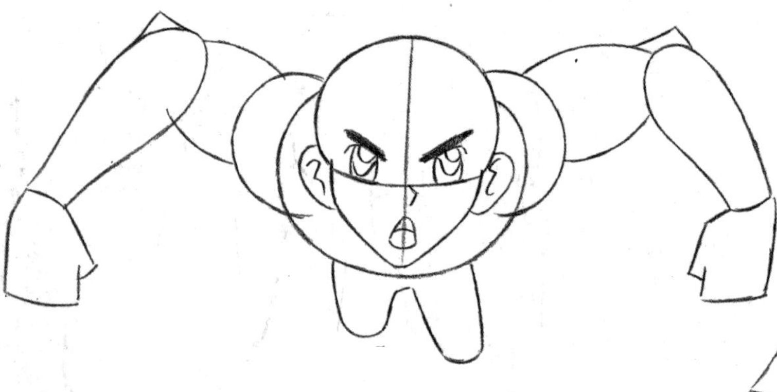

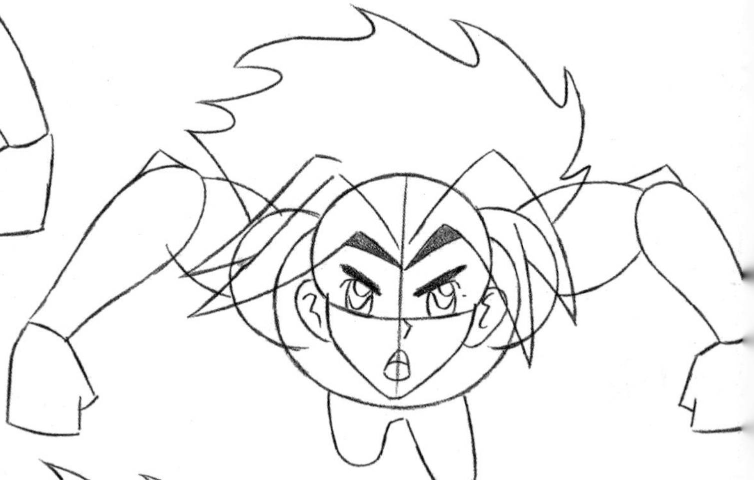

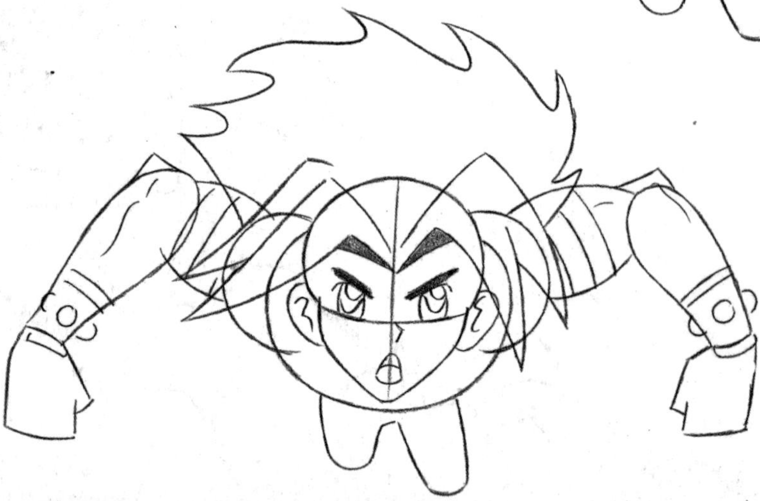

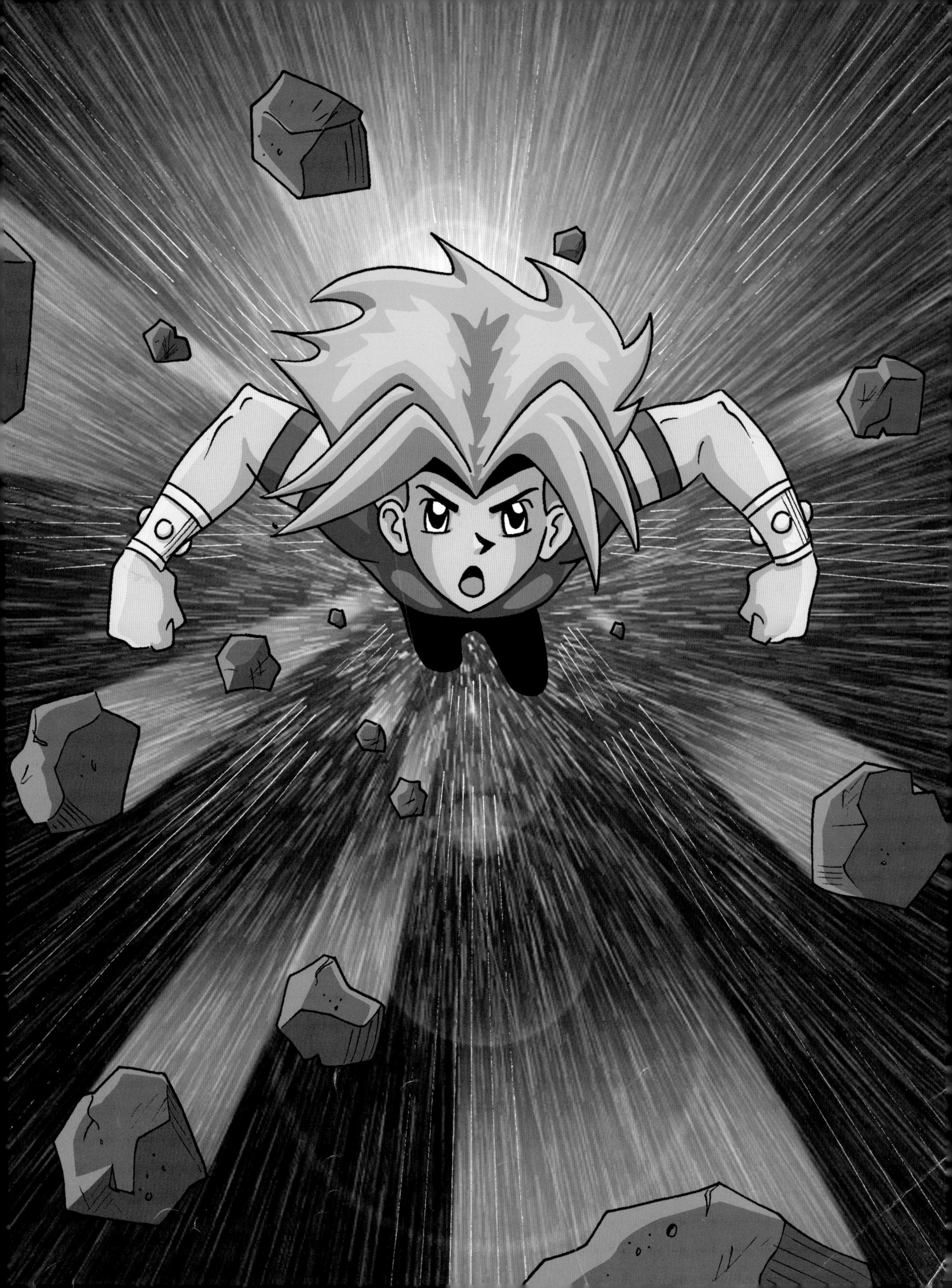

Stylish Girl

This may look like a tough pose to draw, but it's not. That's because the legs and arms are *symmetrical.* This means that both sides are the same. Both legs are in the same position, and both arms are in the same position.

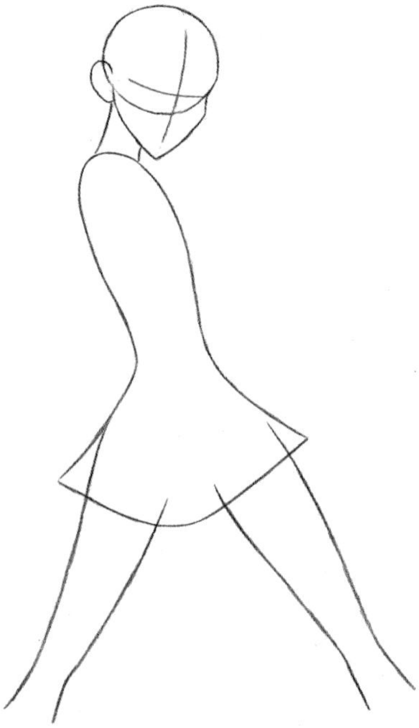

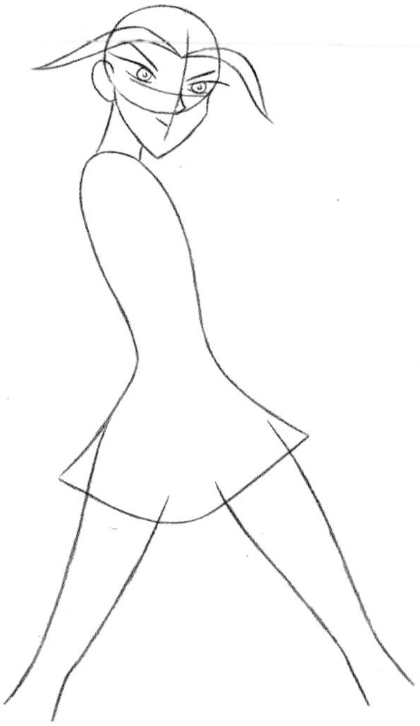

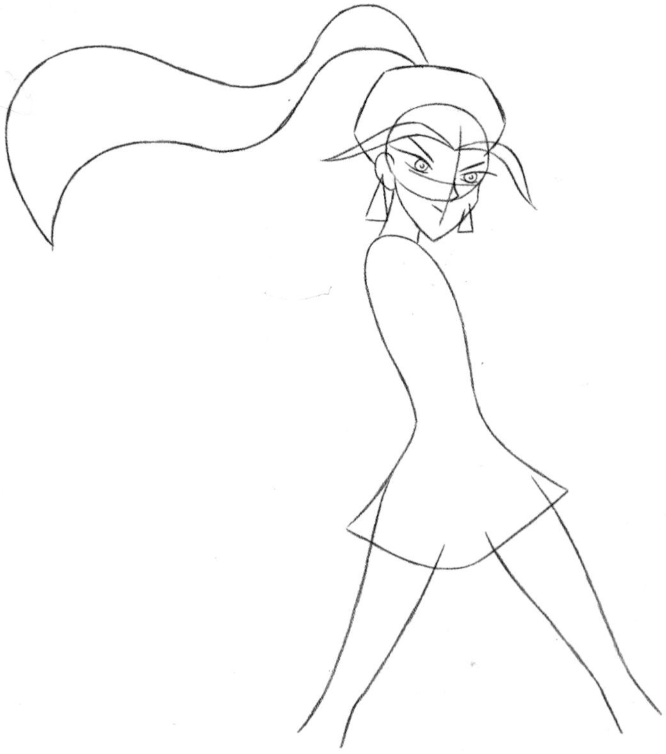

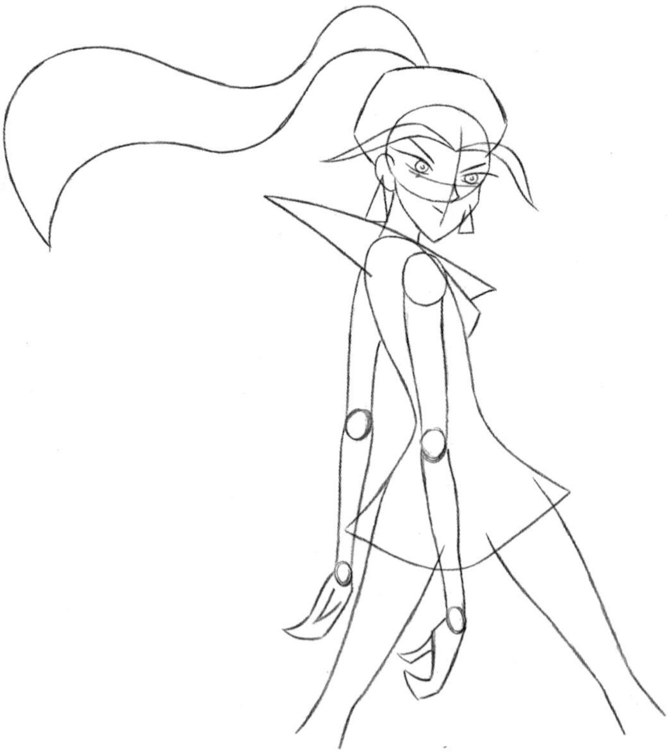

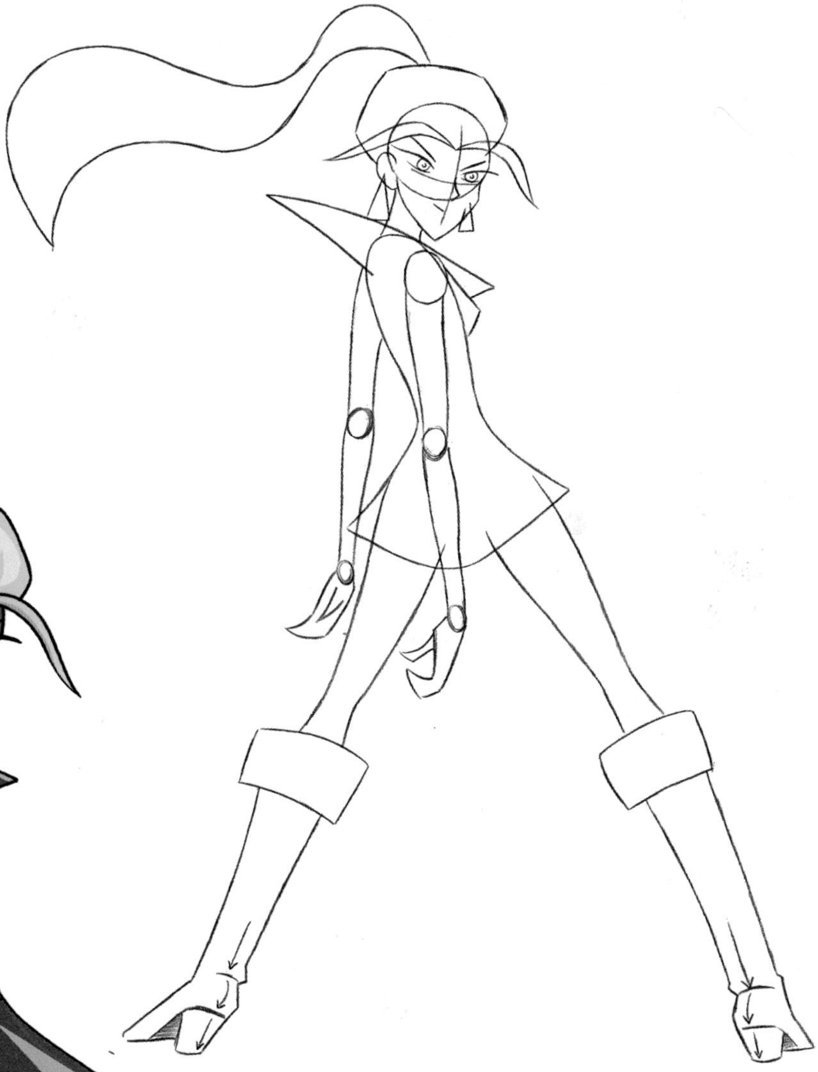

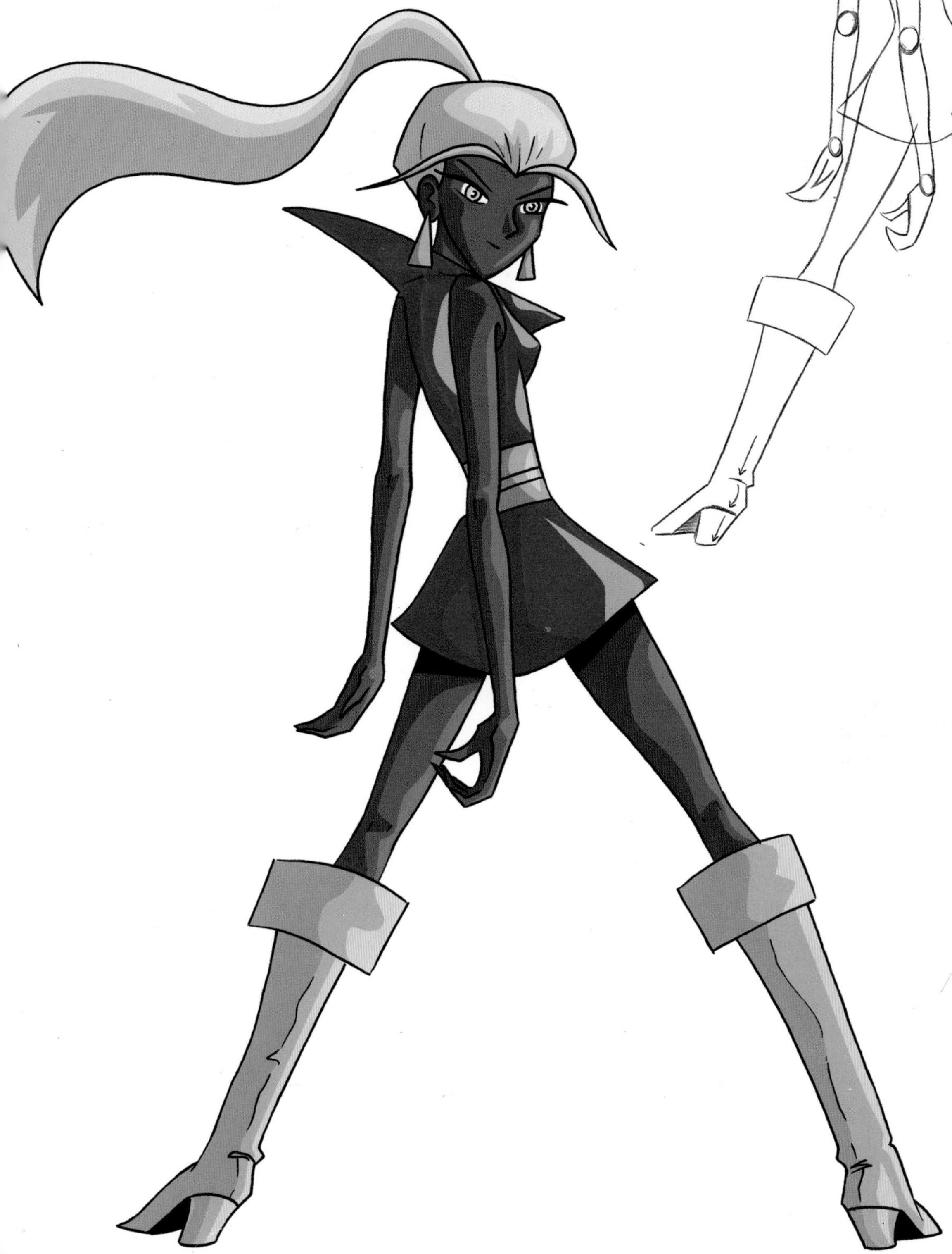

Dark Magic

Manga is a fantasy world where you can let your imagination go wild. Notice how the speed lines make these creatures look like they've just jumped right out of the wizard's hands.

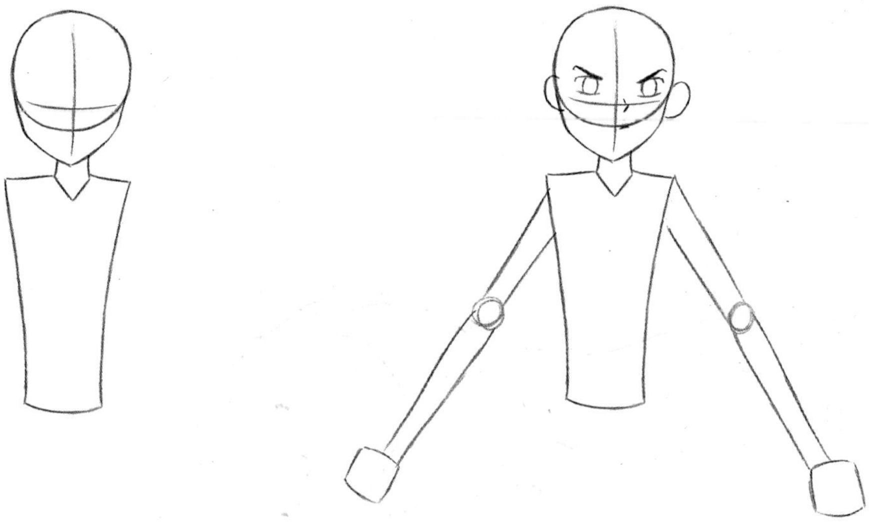

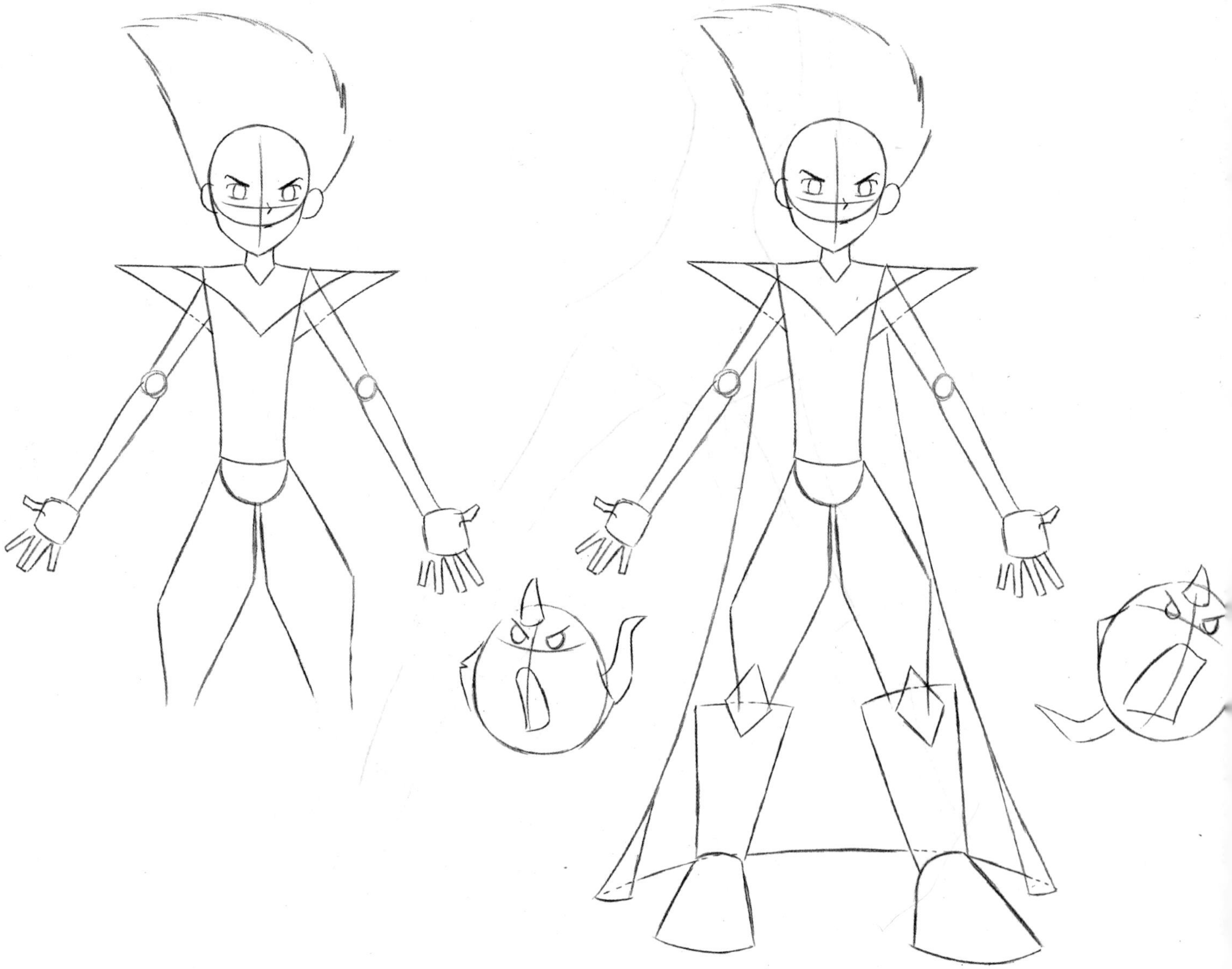

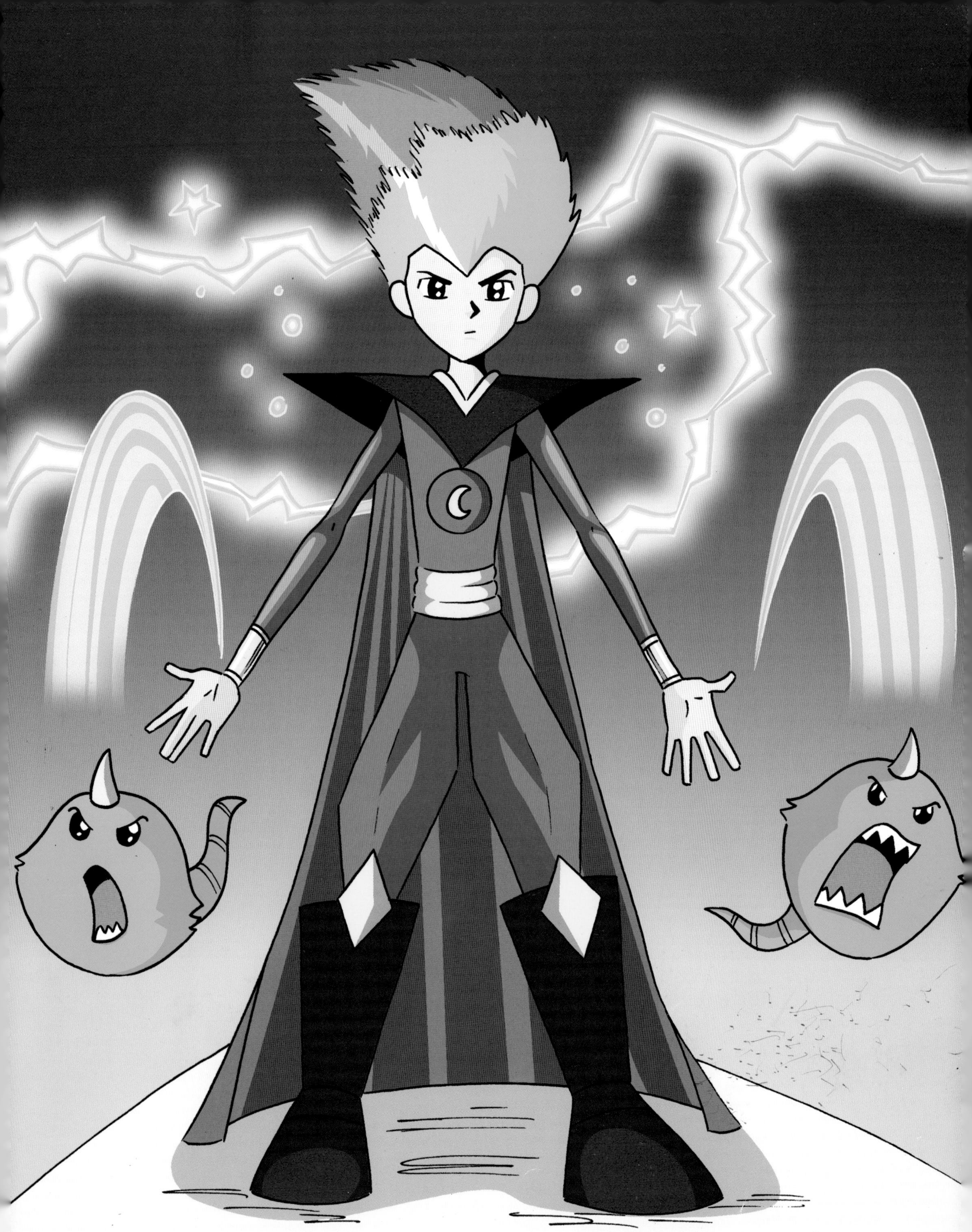

Spaceship Commander

When you design a character, try to come up with an outfit that shows the character's role in the story. What parts of this outfit make her look like a spaceship commander? She's got a jet pack, an insignia on her shoulders (the stars), gloves, kneepads, and—most typical of manga sci-fi characters—big, bulky, futuristic boots.

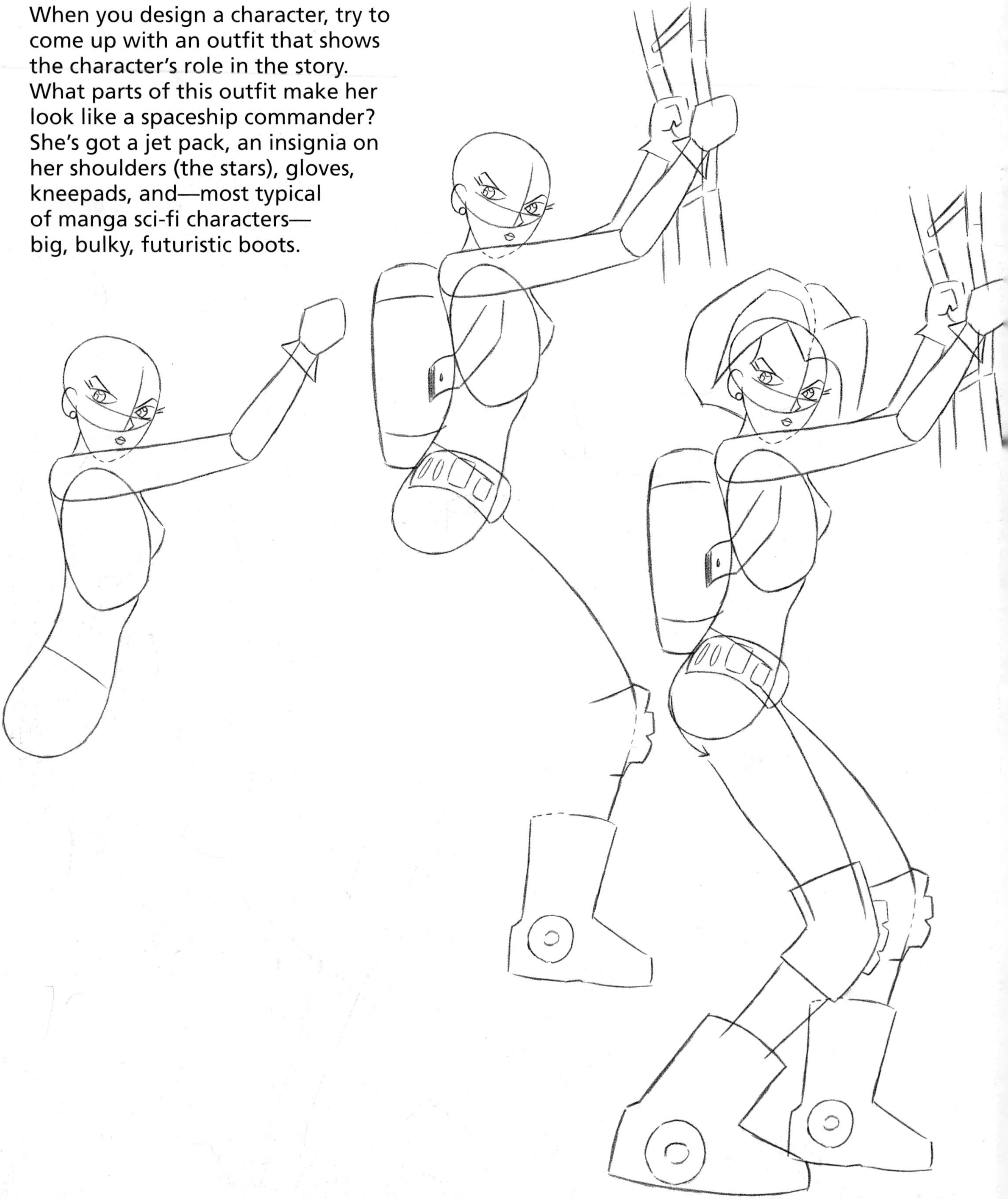

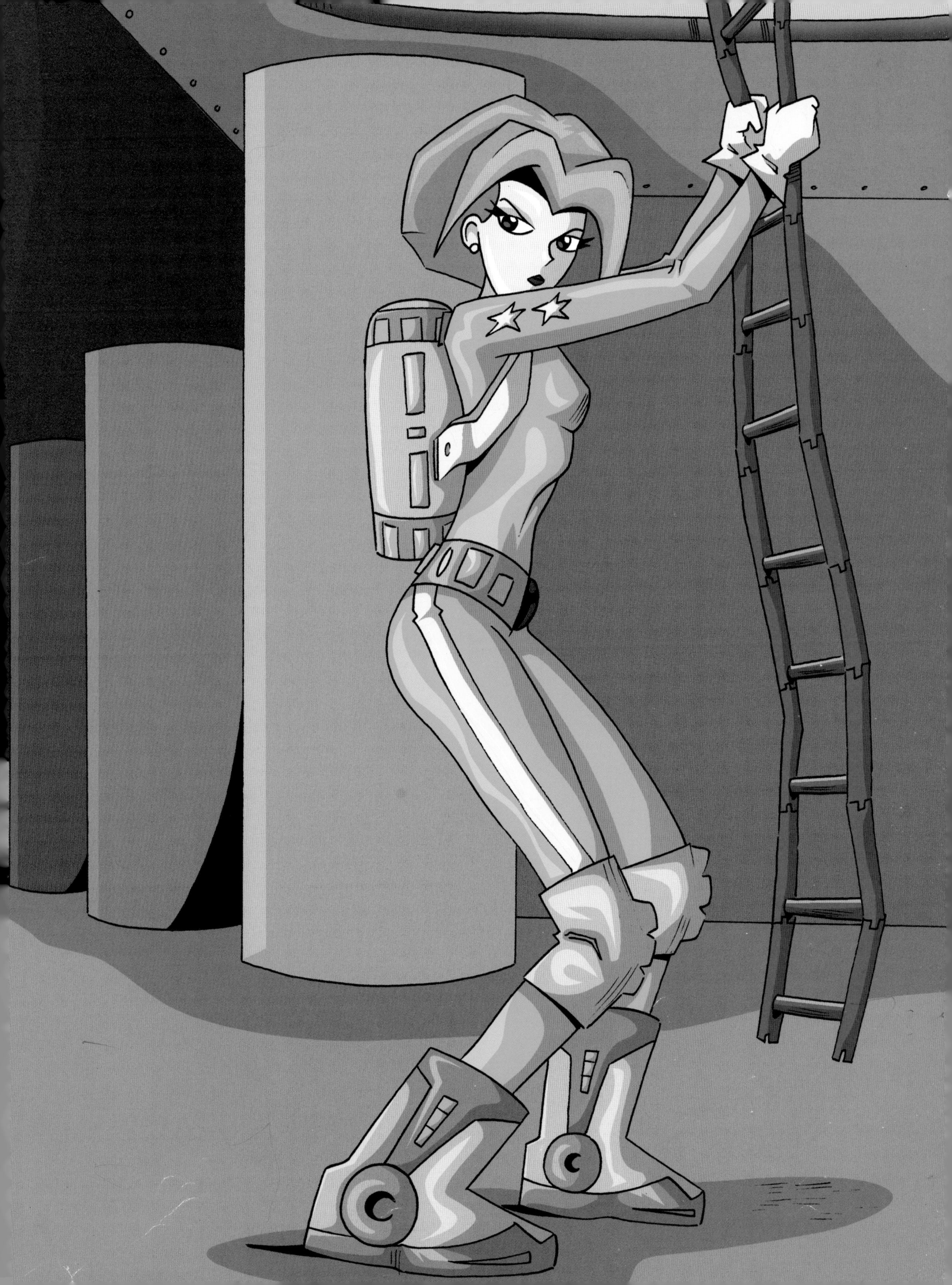

Play Ball!

Artists like to give their characters props to play with. An action as simple as throwing a ball can be turned into a futuristic scene by changing the ball into a mass of highly charged energy.

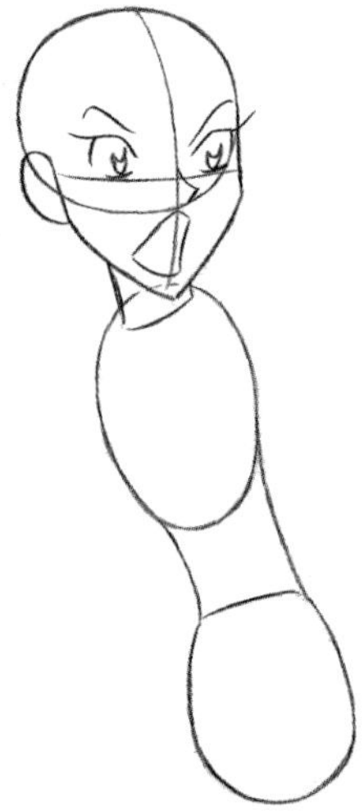

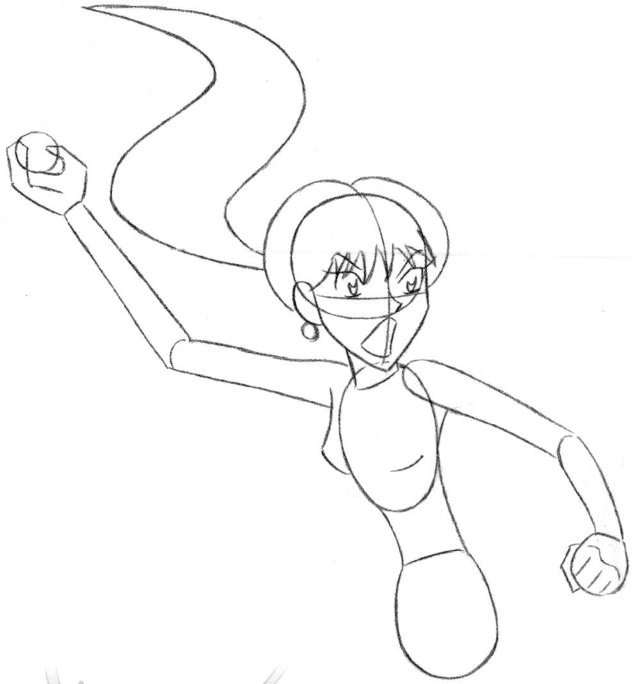

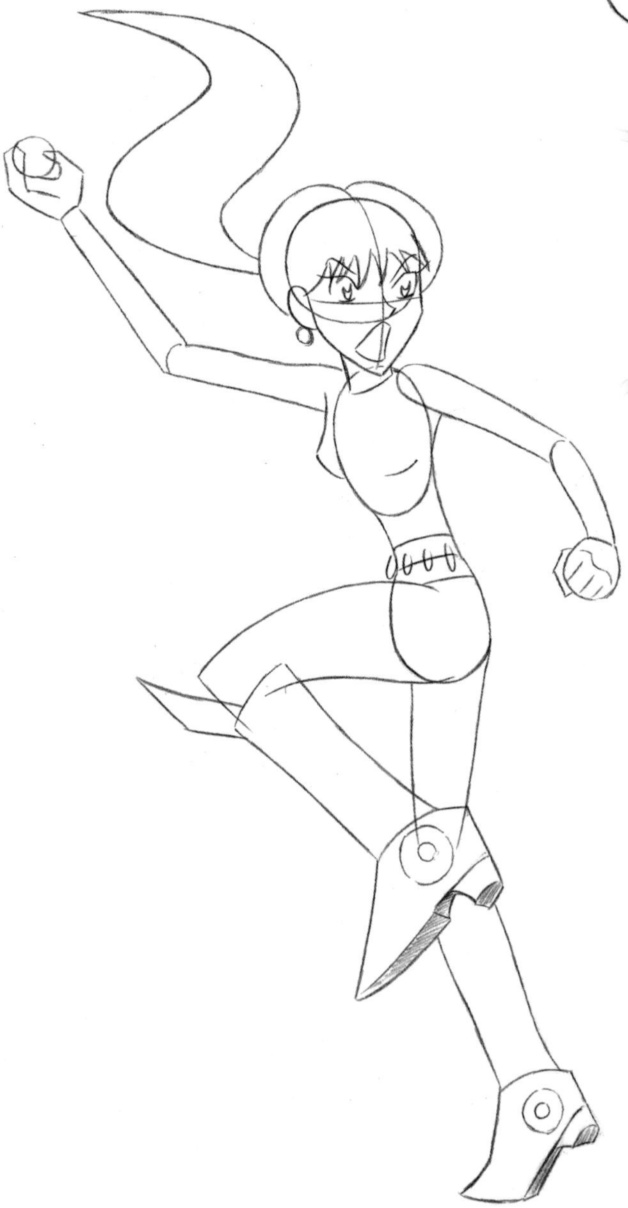

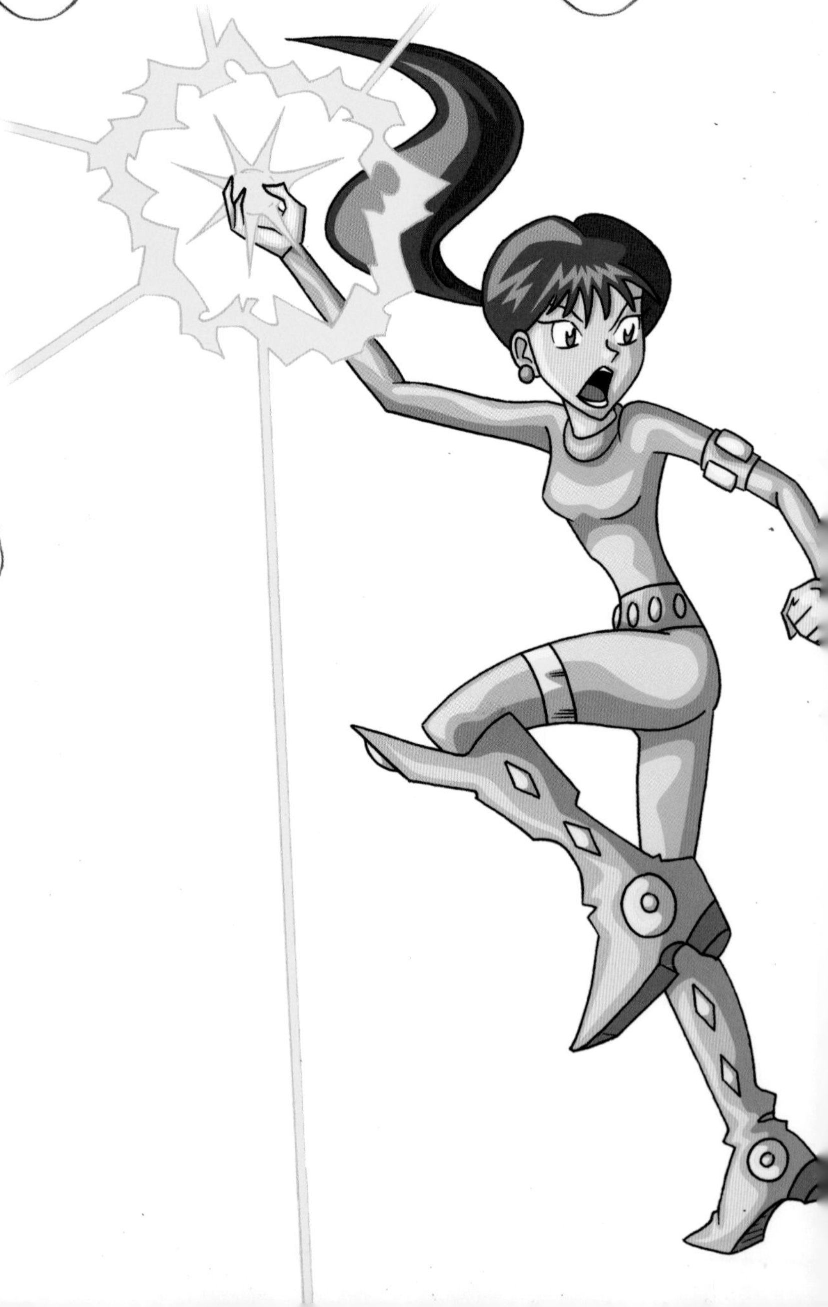

Galaxy Ship Pilot

I've saved a really cool scene for the last picture in the book. It's broken down into lots of steps, so you won't miss a thing as you follow along. Be sure to place the head high up on the page so there's room for the body.

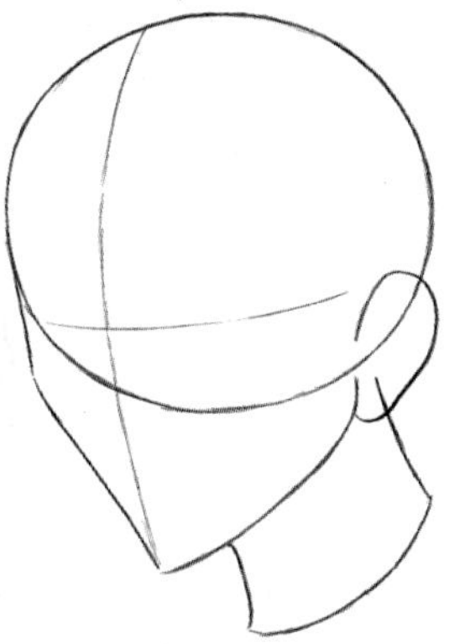

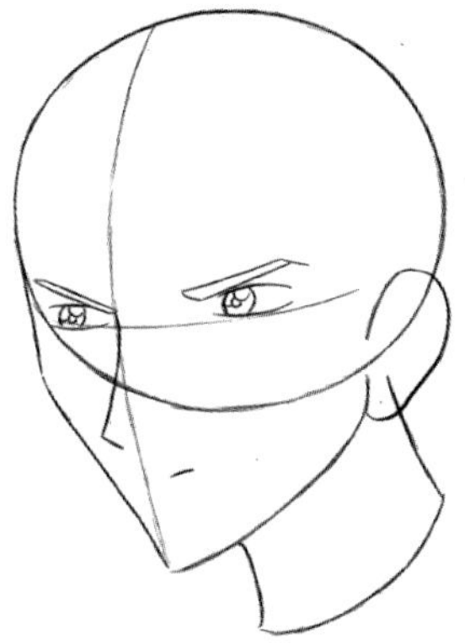

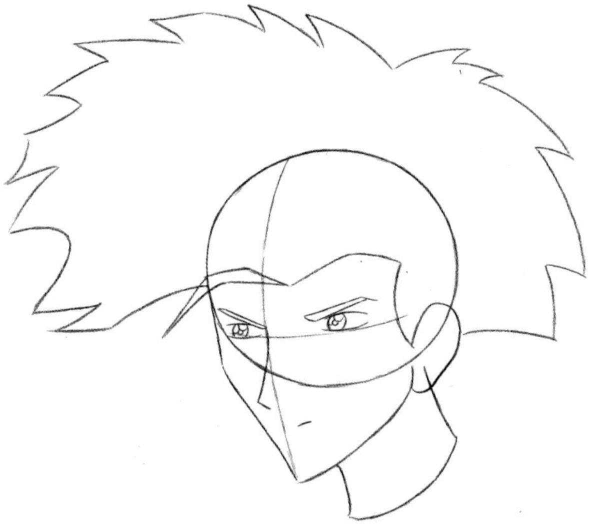

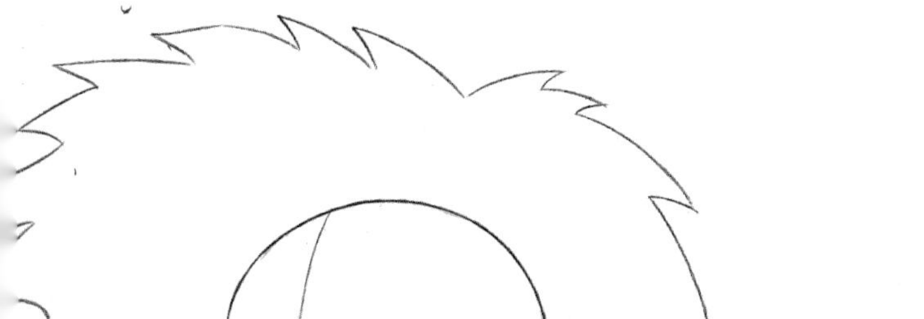

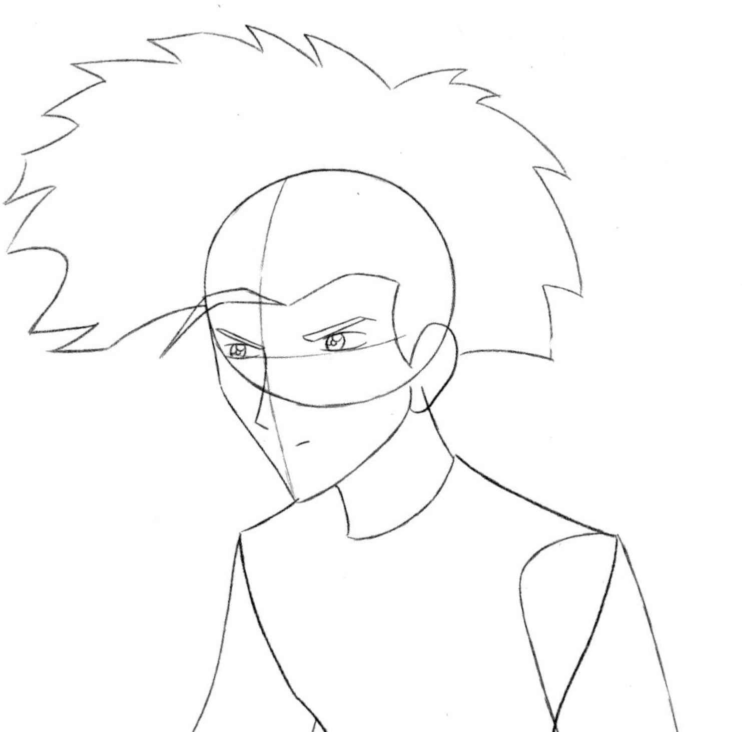

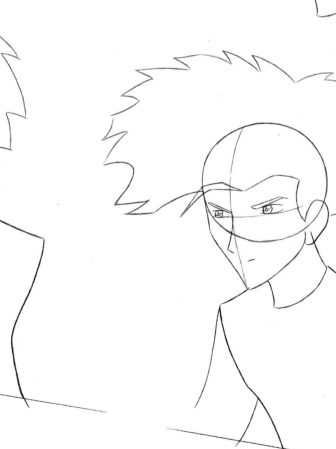

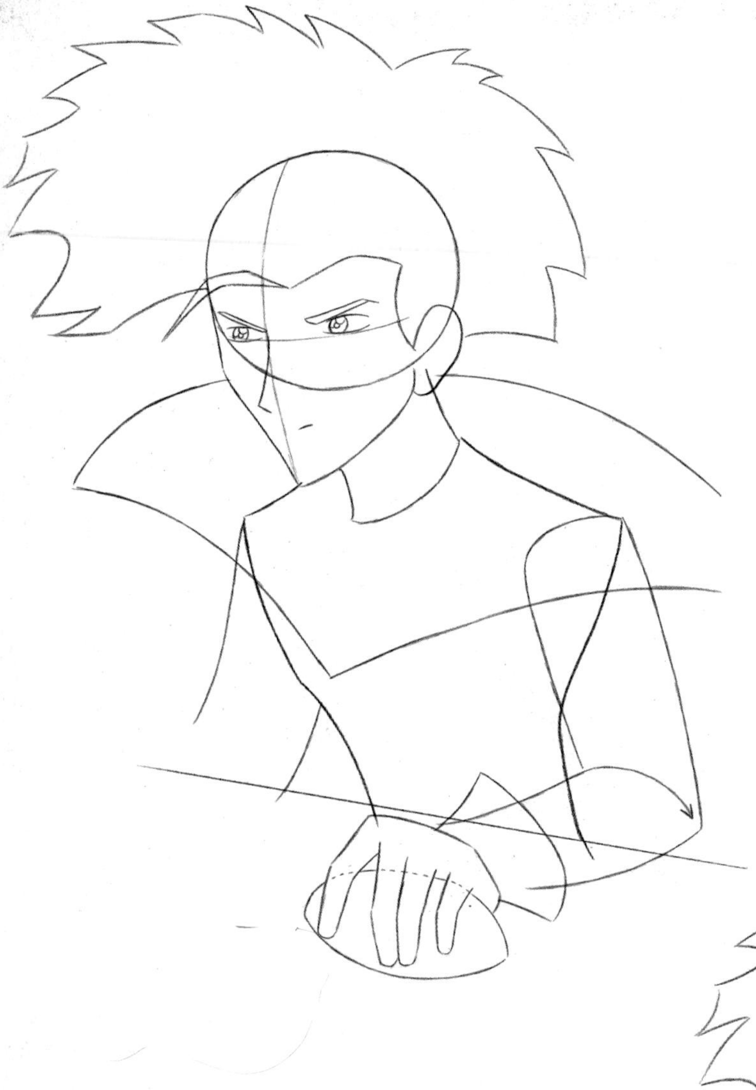

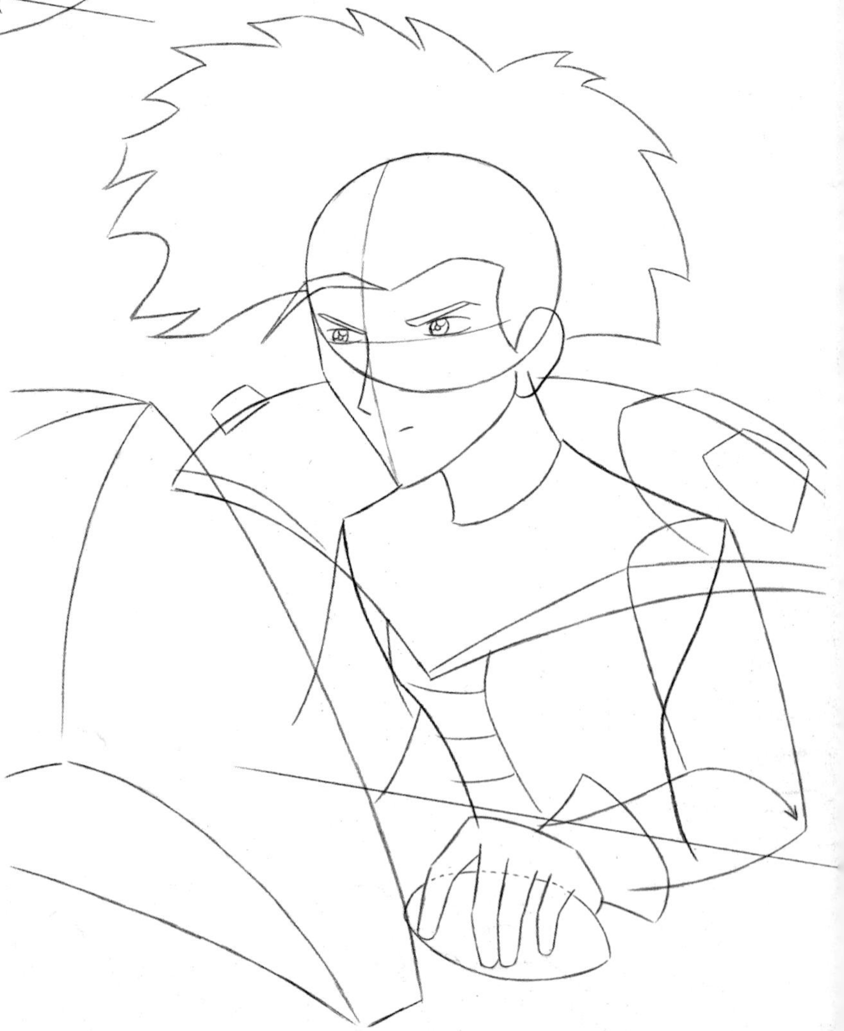

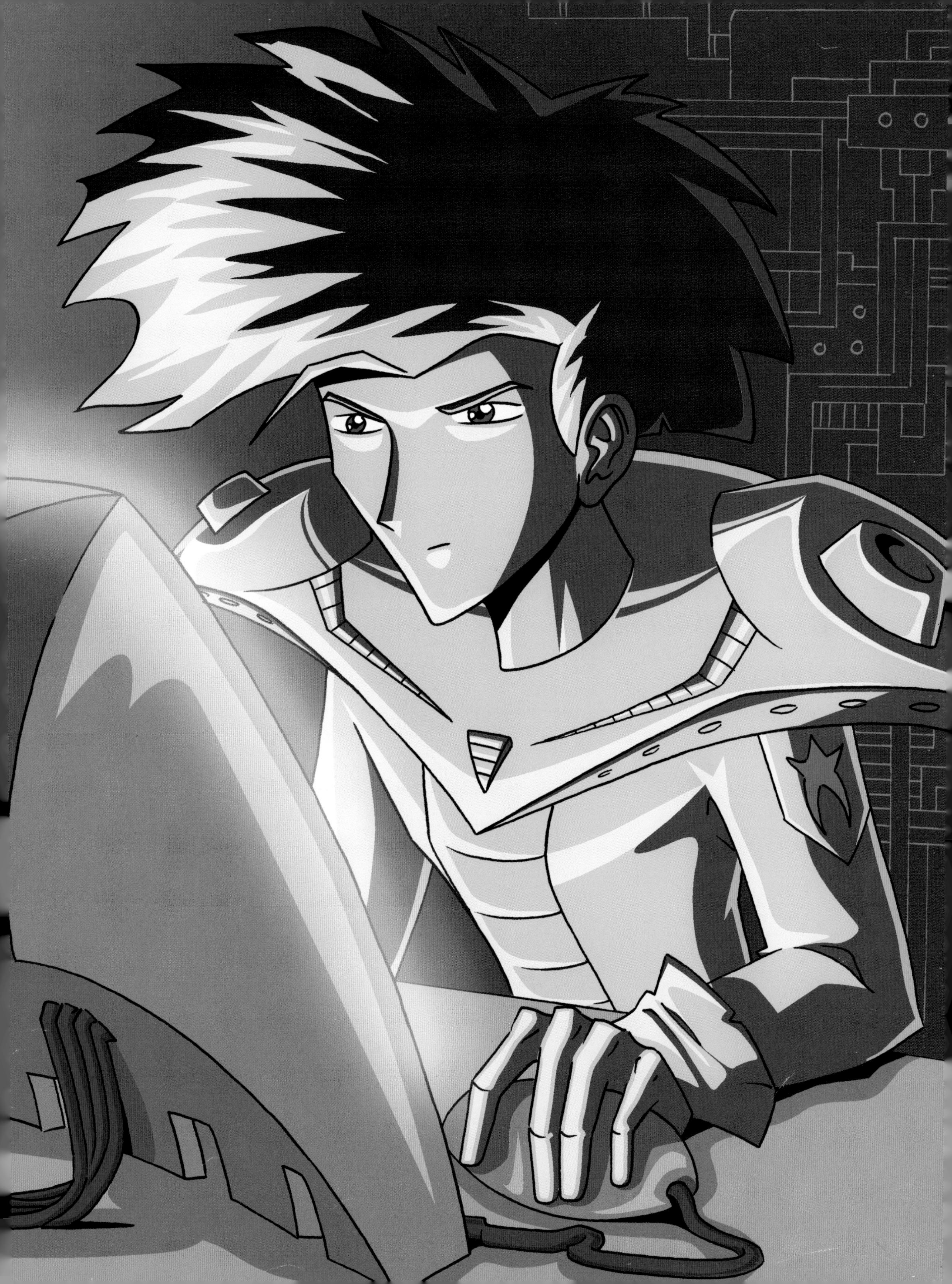

Index

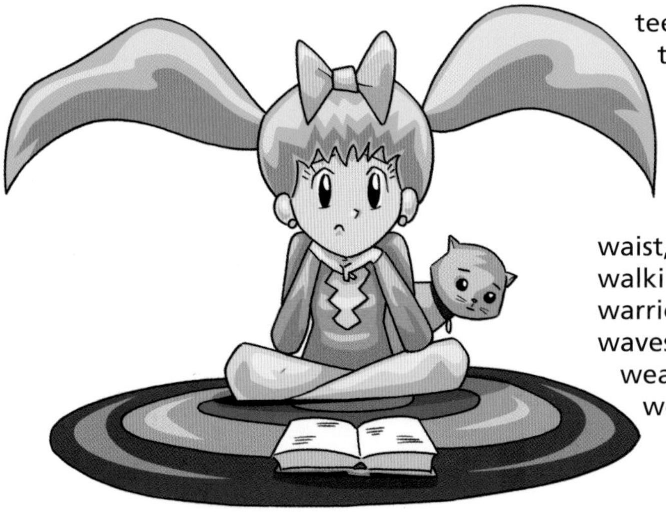